Reading John for Dear Life

A Spiritual Walk with the Fourth Gospel

Jaime Clark-Soles

First edition
Published by Westminster John Knox Press
Louisville, Kentucky

17 18 19 20 21 22 23 24 25—10 9 8 7 6 5 4 3 2

Book design by Sharon Adams
Cover design by Barbara LeVan Fisher / levanfisherstudio.com
Cover art: Margot Clark; margotclark.com (Note from the artist: I am first and foremost a linear artist—lines make up the world! Everything has a focal point from where all ideas and feelings originate. Blues are for water, so soothing, and green is for foliage. Since I am also an avid gardener those two elements are most important to me.)

Library of Congress Cataloging-in-Publication Data

Names: Clark-Soles, Jaime, 1967- author.
Title: Reading John for dear life : a spiritual walk with the fourth gospel / Jaime Clark-Soles.
Description: First edition. | Louisville, KY : Westminster John Knox Press, 2016. | Includes bibliographical references and index.
Identifiers: LCCN 2016009452 (print) | LCCN 2016015077 (ebook) | ISBN 9780664238476 (alk. paper) | ISBN 9781611646955 ()
Subjects: LCSH: Bible. John--Commentaries.
Classification: LCC BS2615.53 .C53 2016 (print) | LCC BS2615.53 (ebook) | DDC 226.5/07--dc23
LC record available at https://lccn.loc.gov/2016009452

♾ The paper used in this publication meets the minimum requirements of the American National Standard for Information Sciences—Permanence of Paper for Printed Library Materials, ANSI Z39.48-1992.

Most Westminster John Knox Press books are available at special quantity discounts when purchased in bulk by corporations, organizations, and special-interest groups. For more information, please e-mail SpecialSales@wjkbooks.com.

To all who have shared my passion for the Gospel of John
and have shaped my reading of it.
You give me life.

Contents

Acknowledgments

I have been studying, teaching, preaching on, loving, and wrestling with the Gospel of John for a long time now. This book is a result of my personal and professional engagement with this text that will not let me go. If I have insights to offer my reader, it will be because of the many wonderful conversation partners I've had over the years, some who love John and some who have their reservations about it (not mutually exclusive categories, of course).

These conversation partners include students who have taken my seminar on John at Perkins School of Theology (some tease me that *every* seminar with me becomes to some extent a seminar on John). That class always fills, and I seem to get the best and the brightest in there. I have shared some of their work and insights in this book. In particular, Beth Taylor has always had a heart for Nicodemus and has pushed me to see him more three-dimensionally than I have in the past. Thanks to the Rev. Lynette Ross, senior minister of Cathedral of Hope Houston UCC, I will never read John 11 in the same way again. The Rev. Cindy Riddick kindly read some of this manuscript and offered helpful suggestions.

I regularly teach in churches of various denominations. I thank all those who have participated in Perkins School for the Laity in Dallas, Houston, Amarillo, Taos, and Alaska. I have to name specifically Susie and Ron Watson; not only did they sit through what ended up being a private session on John for three days in Taos, but they also heard it again in Dallas! And now the next generation of Watsons have joined the study. I thank the Episcopal Diocese of Texas under the leadership of Bishop Andrew C. Doyle, the North

Texas Conference of the United Methodist Church led by Bishop Mike McKee, and the Rio Texas Conference led by Bishop Jim Dorff for the recurring opportunities to address both your laity and your clergy. Of course, my own church, Royal Lane Baptist Church, must be thanked, not only for allowing me to teach there, but more importantly for always challenging me and pushing me to grow.

I have written on John in various places over the years, and here and there I incorporate some of those ideas in the present book. I am a big fan of workingpreacher.org for the way they resource preachers without charge. Some of the ideas related to John 1, 11, 14, 17, and 18 can be found both there and in this book.

In the past few years, I have become involved in Disability Studies as it relates to the Bible. A whole new world has been opened to me, and the learning curve is rather fierce. I am committed to raising awareness whenever possible, for the sake of justice. I have treated Disability Studies and the Johannine Literature at great length in a chapter of *Disability and the Bible: A Commentary,* edited by Sarah Melcher, Amos Yong, Mikeal Parsons (Waco, TX: Baylor University Press, forthcoming). I am grateful to each of those editors for permission to share some of those ideas in an introductory way in chapters 5 and 6 of this book.

The Perkins Scholarly Outreach grant program encourages scholars to share their research and knowledge with an audience larger than their own professional guild. I was fortunate to receive a grant that allowed me to spend time writing this book for a wide audience. I sincerely hope that the goals of that program are furthered by the publication of this book.

I really love big ideas, intense debates, and imagining what could be. Ask me to do logistical things, like citations and formatting and such details, and you will see my energy immediately wane. For that reason, among others, I am deeply grateful for the help of Leslie Fuller, a doctoral candidate in Old Testament/Hebrew Bible at Southern Methodist University for her prompt and patient attention with respect to these matters. It's always good to have a Hebrew Bible scholar by one's side when working on the New Testament!

In that vein, I have to acknowledge my deep good fortune in counting the much beloved and admired Dr. Roy Heller, professor of Old Testament, among my very best friends. I know people are jealous of me for this, as they should be. He's a soul friend who could never be replaced. Not only does he let me share my enthusiasm for John; he adds insights at every turn and multiplies the sense of wonder provoked by Scripture. Maybe this is the best way to convey it: if I die before him, he is in charge of preaching my funeral. Plus, he's handy to have around when you have a pressing Hebrew question and you're under a tight deadline.

Lonnie Brooks directs the Perkins Laity School in Anchorage and attends the Laity School in Dallas each March. He also attends the Society of Biblical Literature meetings; that's pretty hardcore. He graciously read the entire manuscript and offered helpful insights. He is a man of deep faith and intellect who does not suffer fools lightly. I admire him greatly and owe him much.

Anyone keeping track of my publication record will see that I do a lot with Westminster John Knox Press. They are always on the lookout for ways to resource a wide audience, to produce materials that are both smart and timely. For this book, Bridgett Green has been my editor. At every turn she has encouraged me and joined in my excitement for stimulating, meaningful conversations around the Bible. Thanks, Bridgett!

The award for reading this manuscript through multiple times and engaging it in the minutest detail goes to *mi hermana*, my dear soul sister, the Rev. Mireya Martinez. At the risk of sounding maudlin (that joke will make more sense after you read chapter 14), I have to say that she is one of my life's greatest blessings. Our relationship began years ago when she was a school teacher and she showed up to a weekend seminar on John for Laity Week. She then became a Perkins student and is now a stunningly gifted United Methodist minister. Expect to hear more about her and from her in the years ahead. I was also blessed to know her mother, Elma, before she passed away four days before our trip to the Holy Land in January 2015. From Mireya, I continually learn about faith, hope, and love, these three. We might have gone off the Johannine deep end when we noticed recently that she has the same initials as Mary Magdalene and I as Jesus Christ (Superstar). Close friendships give life. Abundant life. Embodied life. Eternal life. Precious life.

Neeki Bey has been my cherished friend for a while now. We first met at an alternative kind of church when he became our music minister—not your ordinary church music minister, let me tell you! He is an astonishingly gifted musician, thinker, and person. Do yourself a favor and learn more about him (neekibey.com). He and I recently had some important conversations about the use of imagery in the tradition that equates sin with blackness and purity with whiteness. A complex topic. You will see some of the fruits of that particular conversation in chapter 3.

Keith Liljestrand—best friend, fellow gym rat, racquetball partner, and running buddy—regularly reminds me that laughter and play (and much trash-talking) are an essential part of life. He is a steady presence in my life; so he's been stuck with lots of conversation about this book in all of its stages. His questions and counsel (whether I heed it or not) always help to clarify my convictions, my goals, and my strategies. His friendship brings me deep joy.

I know I'm too old for a BFF, but I have one anyway. Teri Walker has now seen me through a number of books, not to mention many other life events. I wrote much of this book while sipping from our matching mugs that say "Friend" on one side. The other side says, "We've been through a lot together, and most of it was your fault." I am immensely grateful that, though we share some commonalities, in many ways we view and engage the world very differently. Through it all, I learn and, on my best days, grow in the ways that matter most. I look forward to the next adventure!

My dad, Harold Clark, has taught me about what makes a "real" family and a "real" home. You can read more about that in chapter 9. My mom, Margot Clark, has always taught me through her words and example that if you follow your passion and speak your truth, the rest will fall into place. (I'm not saying that this has made it easy to parent me, especially when I was young.)

I also want to thank my mom for allowing me to use her beautiful glass art piece as the cover of my book. When I saw it, I knew it fit the imagery of the Gospel perfectly. I've always admired her artistic ability, which I did not inherit; she kindly insists that words are my art (you know how moms are): what holy ground it is for me, then, to combine our efforts for the sake of the Gospel. Thanks, Mom!

My mother-in-law, Caroline Soles, is a paragon of faithfulness and self-sacrificial love. I dedicate chapter 8 to her. If I ever, in this lifetime, come to practice one iota of what is preached in those chapters, it will be because I've watched her long enough to imagine putting it into practice. Where she is Mary of Bethany, I find myself being Judas. But there is surely hope for me, if only because I know she prays for me regularly and the prayers of the righteous "availeth much" (Jas. 5:16 KJV).

Finally, my deepest gratitude must always go to my husband and children, who make possible this life and this work that I love so much. I'm not sure what Thad imagined he signed up for back when we were just college kids at Stetson University, hanging out at the BCM (Baptist Campus Ministry), but he has made space for all of my dreams for close to three decades now. His love and his commitment to our family sustain me. Grace, Chloe, and Caleb continue to inspire, challenge, and humble me. They are robust conversation partners with their own sense of self and their own ideas (even when I find that inconvenient and tell them so). They make me think in new ways. They humor me. They love me. Surely not as much as I love them? Sheer gift.

Every last bit of all of it—grace upon grace.

Jaime Clark-Soles
Dallas, TX
September 2015

Chapter 1

Your One Wild and Precious (and Abundant) Life

Overview

Welcome to the Gospel of John! Whether this is your first time ever laying eyes on this text or your hundredth time, all manner of marvels await you. The Gospel has twenty-one chapters, each one rich and dense with meaning, comfort, and challenge. While we won't be able to engage all twenty-one chapters in depth here, I've chosen some of the highlights to help focus our reading, study, prayer, and discussion. The reader will notice that some chapters have prayers, meditations, or study questions, but not all do. My explanation? The Spirit moves where it wills (John 3:8), so I followed where it led, rather than trying to capture and contain it. The Holy Spirit is not a genie in a bottle.

Certainly, you'll want to read (and reread) the whole Gospel and note your own questions and insights about anything you find. I am simply here to guide you and inspire you to devote time to the Word of and from God in John that you will find for your own spiritual walk. One note before we begin: all quotations of the biblical text come from the New Revised Standard Version, unless otherwise noted. You will notice that I pick fights with the NRSV from time to time—not because it's a bad translation, but because *all* translations fall short in one way or another.

To start, take a moment to answer this set of questions briefly. Tell me something about John that you

- think,
- feel,
- know, and
- wonder about.

Keep that list by you as we proceed through our study.

Tradition assigns the eagle as the symbol for the Gospel of John because only the soaring eagle can stare straight into the sun. Clement of Alexandria, a second-century church leader, said this: "Last of all, John, perceiving that the external facts had been made plain in the [other] Gospels, and being urged by his friends and inspired by the Spirit, composed a spiritual Gospel" (Eusebius, *Ecclesiastical History* 6.14.5–7). Another sage describes John as shallow enough for a child to wade in, deep enough for an elephant to swim in. We aim to discover the richness of this Gospel, whose uniqueness and layers of mystery continue to grip its readers and whose unanticipated surprises delight at every turn. We expect to be transformed.

John doesn't make us guess why he or she[1] wrote this Gospel: "But these things are written so that y'all [you all, plural] may come to believe that Jesus is the Messiah, the Son of God, and that through believing y'all may have life in his name" (20:31, my trans.).

Everything from 1:1 through 21:25[2] was written not merely to *inform* us, but to *transform* us. John does not aim to provide an objective account of people and events in order to add another tome to the annals of human history. No, this is persuasive speech; and if this Gospel has its way with us, we will feel directly addressed by God in Christ and receive the abundant life that belongs to us as members of God's own family.

Life is a favorite theme in this Gospel. Many people know John 3:16 by heart, usually in the King James Version: "For God so loved the world that he gave his only begotten Son, that whosoever believeth in him should not perish, but have everlasting life." And in

1. The debate about the authorship of this Gospel is lively, layered, and ongoing. The Gospel does not say who wrote it. Many authors have been suggested, some male and some female. For a solid discussion of the topic, see Sandra Schneiders, *Written That You May Believe* (New York: Crossroad, 2003), 233–54, and Paul Anderson, *The Riddles of the Fourth Gospel* (Minneapolis: Fortress Press, 2011), 95–124. I will refer to the author as "he" or "John" in this book, not because I assume that the author is male but for the sake of convenience.

2. John has a rich composition history, including two endings—the first being chap. 20 and the second chap. 21. Some would call chap. 21 an appendix. For the most thorough academic treatment of the composition of the Gospel of John and the Epistles of John, see Urban von Wahlde's work in three volumes: *The Gospel and Letters of John* (Grand Rapids: Eerdmans, 2010). For an excellent shorter treatment, see Paul Anderson, *The Riddles of the Fourth Gospel* (Minneapolis: Fortress Press, 2011), 95–124.

John 10:10 (NRSV), Jesus declares, "I came that they may have life, and have it abundantly."

In fact, the word "life" (*zōē*) is used thirty-six times in John. The verb (*zaō*) occurs seventeen times. There's even another verb, to "give life or make alive" (*zōopoieō*), that occurs three times and *only* in the Fourth Gospel. The Gospel actually begins with life. In the Prologue to John (1:1–18), we hear, "All things came into being through him, and without him not one thing came into being. What has come into being in him was *life*, and the *life* was the light of all people."

The fact that the Word helped to create all that exists reminds us that we should take a look around us, at everything in the world, and see how the created order might connect us to God and teach us something about what abundant life looks like. Clearly, abundant life isn't primarily about the *length* of our lives but rather the *quality* of our lives. It's about living a certain kind of life, for however long that may last.

William Sloane Coffin, longtime pastor of the Riverside Church in New York, put it this way: "While Abraham lived through 'summer's parching heat,' Jesus died young; but didn't both show us that it is by its content rather than by its duration that a lifetime is measured?"[3] And again: "Deserted by his disciples, in agony on the cross, barely thirty years old, Christ said, 'It is finished.' And thus ended the most complete life ever lived."[4]

Mary Oliver is a poet after John's own heart. Her poem "The Summer Day" fits the Gospel of John perfectly as she asks, "Who made the world?" She reminds us how to observe the world prayerfully and, finally, confronts us with the question of all questions:

> Doesn't everything die at last, and too soon?
> Tell me, what is it you plan to do
> with your one wild and precious life?[5]

John asks us the very same question. John calls us to slow down, to pay attention, and to get a life, an abundant one marked by the eternal.

3. William Sloane Coffin, *Credo* (Louisville, KY: Westminster John Knox Press, 2004), Kindle edition.

4. Coffin, *Credo*.

5. Mary Oliver, *House of Light* (Boston: Beacon Press, 1990), 60.

You could say that John is concerned with nothing but life: how we get it, how we lose it, how we find it again—or better yet, how we get found by it. Abundant life, embodied life, eternal life, precious life.

Some Things to Notice as You Go: Tips for Reading

John bears reading over and over again. As a fellow traveler, I offer the following as signposts.

1. Pay attention to the special repetitive vocabulary, such as light and darkness, life, truth, world, word, witness, testify, and family language (children, birth, womb, father, mother).

2. A key feature of the Fourth Gospel is the use of "I am" statements. We will address the specific occurrences as they arise, but you need to know from the start that there are two kinds of "I am" statements in John (for a great chart, see Felix Just's "*I Am*" *Sayings in the Fourth Gospel* site: http://catholic-resources.org/John/Themes-IAM.htm).

First, there are the "I am" statements followed by a predicate nominative:

- I am the bread of life (6:35, 41, 48, 51).
- I am the light of the world (8:12; 9:5).
- I am the gate of the sheepfold (10:7, 9).
- I am the good shepherd (10:11, 14).
- I am the resurrection and the life (11:25).
- I am the way and the truth, that is, the life (14:6).
- I am the true vine (15:1, 5).

Second, there are the absolute "I am" statements, where Jesus says only "I am" (*egō eimi*), playing off of God's own self-designation in the Old Testament as evidenced in Exodus 3:14 (See, e.g., John 4:26; 6:20; 8:24, 28, 58; 13:19; 18:5–8).

3. Notice the extremely intimate personal encounters between Jesus and individual characters. Some of the characters we know only from John. In other places, we see characters we know from other Gospels, but they are having experiences narrated only in John. For example:

- Nathaniel (chap. 1)
- Jesus' mother (chap. 2)
- Nicodemus (chap. 3)
- the Samaritan woman (chap. 4)
- the man ill for thirty-eight years (chap. 5)
- the man born blind (chap. 9)
- Mary, Martha, and Lazarus (chap. 11)
- Mary (the sister of Martha and Lazarus) (chap. 12)
- Judas (chaps. 12 and 13)
- Pilate (chap. 19)
- Mary Magdalene at the cross (chap. 19), at the tomb, and in the garden (chap. 20)
- Peter on the beach (chap. 21)

4. John could be called the "Gospel of intimate, touchy relationships"; there is no more intimate book in the Bible than the Gospel of John. Jesus and God and the Holy Spirit and we are all intimately related to one another. It's a very touchy Gospel: Jesus rubs mud on the blind man's eyes; Mary anoints Jesus' feet and wipes them with her hair; Jesus washes the disciples' dirty feet; Mary Magdalene grabs onto the resurrected Jesus as he is about to ascend. We could easily multiply the instances of intimacy in this Gospel, but I want to draw your attention to one in particular.

In 1:18 John tells us that Jesus is in the "breast" (*kolpos*) of the Father. Some translations translate *kolpos* here as "heart" (New Jerusalem Bible, NRSV). Others go with "at his side" (English Standard Version, New American Bible). Both are unhelpful and misleading. First, we have a word for heart: *kardia*. But *kardia* does not appear here. Second, the only other place *kolpos* appears in John is 13:23, where the Beloved Disciple was reclining *upon* Jesus' breast, not *next* to him. John wants us to understand that the kind of intimacy between God and Jesus also exists between us and Jesus/God. The mistranslation obscures this fact. If you are uncomfortable with touching, with the stuff of earth, with the eradication of lines between the so-called "mundane" and the so-called "sacred," I suggest that you take up another text. John will not countenance such a separation. Hence, the incarnation.

5. Matthew, Mark, and Luke are known as the Synoptic Gospels because they share a close literary relationship such that they can be

"viewed together," *syn-optic*. If you are familiar with the Synoptic Gospels, you may think of Peter as the "star" of the disciples. In John, it's the Beloved Disciple ("the one whom Jesus loved" in the NRSV). While many people assume this is John, son of Zebedee, you must note that the text never names this disciple. Interpreters have suggested many people, including Lazarus, Mary Magdalene, and Jesus' brother James. Let's honor the fact that the author never names the Beloved Disciple. In making that choice, the author expects *you* and *me*, readers and hearers of this text, to insert ourselves into that very slot. The Beloved Disciple always "gets it right." By the time we're done with the Fourth Gospel, the author expects *us* to be that disciple.

6. E. B. White, author of *Charlotte's Web*, once said: "I arise in the morning torn between a desire to improve (or save) the world and a desire to enjoy (or savor) the world. This makes it hard to plan the day."[6] I can relate to that so well. Can you? The Fourth Gospel certainly can; it expresses a conflicted relationship with the world. On the one hand, there is no doubt that God and Jesus created the world (see the Prologue) and that they aim to save it (3:16–17). On the other hand, the world "hates" Jesus, and his disciples should anticipate the same experience (15:18–19). On the one hand, the world is associated with Satan; one of John's favorite names for Satan is "the ruler of this world" (12:31; 14:30; 16:11). On the other hand, when he talks about Satan, it's usually to discuss how Satan's number is up: he has no power over Jesus; he stands condemned.

7. Every intimate personal encounter with Jesus has the power to transform us, but that transformation is *always* worked out in the context of community. There is no "Lone Ranger" Christianity in John (or anywhere in Scripture, for that matter, but that's another story).

8. John is a narrative, not a newspaper account. Respect it as such. Read it in one sitting or watch the movie *The Gospel of John* (narrated by Christopher Plummer). Allow yourself to enter fully into the narrative world that John has created. Shut out all else during that time. It will take you three hours to watch the movie, start to finish,

6. Quoted in a profile by Israel Shenker, "E. B. White: Notes and Comment by Author," *New York Times*, July 11, 1969.

word for word. Enter the characters as if you were they. Try them all on for size. You might ask yourself the following as you do this:

- What strikes you in this passage?
- Do you like or dislike the character in this story? Why or why not?
- Do you like or dislike Jesus in this story? Why or why not?
- What previous experience or relationship do you have with this piece of Scripture? Have you heard it preached? How does that shape your understanding of it now?
- Where does it intersect with your own life? For instance, the Samaritan woman had needs, and she asked according to those particular needs: "Give me water." What are your needs? What do you want to say to Jesus in place of "Give me this water"?
- What does it teach us about the kind of community our church should or could be?

9. John is quite different from the Synoptic Gospels. Do not try to "fix" John by imposing their narrative or theology upon John. At times I will, in fact, compare John with the Synoptics, not to fix any of them, but rather (a) to show John's distinctiveness or (b) to clear up any confusion that may exist due to readers' bringing the Synoptic version to the story. For instance, if I ask you to picture the scene of Jesus carrying his cross, most readers will image Simon of Cyrene helping Jesus. But in John, Jesus carries his cross alone. That's not just an interesting difference; it's a crucial one for understanding John's theology, particularly John's Christology (the understanding of Jesus' life and work).

10. It's quite useful to read one character in light of other characters. I call this intercharacterization. So read the Samaritan woman in contrast to and comparison with *both* Nicodemus, who precedes her, and the disciples, who show up after her encounter with Jesus (in which she becomes the first broad evangelist). Read the story of the man who is ill in chapter 5 in comparison with the Samaritan woman in chapter 4 *and* the man born blind in chapter 9. Read the Samaritan woman in comparison to the man born blind (hint: both of them are heroes in this Gospel, modeling what we, the readers, should be like). And so on.

11. I usually teach my John class over a semester. Each week, we begin the class with a prayer, song, or some other centering exercise.

Then we share what I call "Johannine moments"—any experiences the participants have had where the text intersected with their lives. When you immerse yourself in very particular Scriptures for a set time, it's surprising the ways connections arise. I invite you then to keep an eye out for your own Johannine moments during your study.

The Word, Embodied

For John, abundant, eternal life is, above all, *embodied* life. Bodies are good. Creation is good. How could they not be, since God made all of it? The Gospel opens with creation, drawing upon language from the first creation story, found in the opening of Genesis:

> In the beginning when God created the heavens and the earth, the earth was a formless void and darkness covered the face of the deep, while a wind from God swept over the face of the waters. Then God said, "Let there be light"; and there was light. And God saw that the light was good. (Gen. 1:1–4)

> In the beginning was the Word, and the Word was with God, and the Word was God. He was in the beginning with God. All things came into being through him, and without him not one thing came into being. What has come into being in him was life, and the life was the light of all people. The light shines in the darkness, and the darkness did not overcome/comprehend it. (John 1:1–5)

If we are going to take John seriously, then we are going to have to take creation, and our embodiedness, seriously:

> If the Word of God became flesh and dwelt among us—that is, if the Word of God came out of the birth canal of a woman's body, grew, ate, went to the bathroom, bathed, struggled against demons, sweated, wept, exulted, was transfigured, was physically violated, and rotted away in a tomb just before being gloriously resurrected—then the Bible must have flesh on it. If a valley of dry bones can live again, then bones and blood and bread and flesh and bodies should never be left behind when we are trying to understand the grime and glory of Scripture. Any interpretation that denounces the material, created order, including our own bodies, should be suspect. From birth to death our bodies swell and shrink;

> they are wet with milk and sweat and urine and vomit and sex and blood and water, and wounds that fester and stink and are healed and saved and redeemed and die and are resurrected. If you can't glory in or at least talk about these basic realities in church while reading Scripture, then how can Scripture truly intersect with or impact life?[7]

If you know Genesis well, you will see many other instances where John draws from it. In fact, this Gospel is famous for its use of the Old Testament.[8] The author was steeped in Scripture. Not a bad idea for all people in any century, really.

Structure of the Gospel

John is sometimes called "the maverick Gospel" because it differs from its Gospel counterparts. You can see this from the way each Gospel begins. Mark starts with Jesus' baptism. Matthew moves it back to a genealogy and a visit from an angel to righteous Joseph, followed by the birth of Jesus. Luke kicks it back to John the Baptist and his parents; the annunciation to Mary; the special meeting between two exceptional women, Elizabeth and Mary; and the census and birth of Jesus, made famous to modern Americans by Linus's performance in "A Charlie Brown Christmas" or by children's Christmas pageants every December.

The Fourth Gospel begins with a Prologue (1:1–18). Chapters 1–12 are known as the Book of Signs. In these chapters, Jesus conducts his public ministry and enacts seven "signs" (*semeia*). Never does John use the word so familiar from the Synoptics when they refer to "miracles" (*dynameis*). Signs point to something. The signs in John are used to point to Jesus' identity as Messiah, the child of God, sent by God and acting with all the agency of God. Chapters 13–20 are known as the Book of Glory. Here Jesus turns away from his public ministry to focus upon the disciples. He models for them servant leadership in the footwashing. In the Farewell Discourse

7. Jaime Clark-Soles, *Engaging the Word* (Louisville, KY: Westminster John Knox Press, 2010), 32.

8. For a detailed treatment, see Clark-Soles, *Scripture Cannot Be Broken* (Leiden: E. J. Brill, 2003).

(chaps. 14–17), Jesus consoles them in their anxiety and fear related to his physical departure and prays for their/our unity. The passion and resurrection occupy chapters 18–20. Chapter 21 addresses, among other things, the rehabilitation/reconciliation of Peter, who, under heat by a warm fire, coldly denied Jesus.

That the Gospel has two endings is obvious if one reads the conclusions of chapters 20 and 21. Scholars debate whether the same author penned the second ending at a later date or whether another hand is responsible for that. In fact, the Gospel of John has a layered composition history, so that question arises in various places within the narrative. As interesting and important as that conversation may be, it's a side issue with respect to the goals of this particular book.

No matter which ending resonates with you, one thing is clear: the author is calling us as individuals and as communities to be addressed by this Gospel. The rabbis have a saying that fits this Gospel perfectly: "Turn it and turn it [the Torah] again, for everything is in it; and contemplate it and grow grey and old over it and stir not from it" (Mishnah *Avot* 5:22).[9] Now is the time.

9. This quotation comes from part of the Mishnah called the *Pirkei Avot* (Sayings of the Fathers), which is composed of a variety of ethical maxims attributed to a long line of rabbis and other leaders. One translation of this chapter can be found online at http://www.jewishvirtuallibrary.org/jsource/Talmud/avot5.html. As with other Hebrew documents, it uses letters rather than numbers to designate sections, so 5:22 is 5:FF in this translation.

Chapter 2

In the Beginning

John 1

Prayer: God of life, light, and love, help us to know your truth, the truth that sets us free.

The Prologue

The Prologue (1:1–18) introduces the major themes of the Gospel. Stop what you are doing, read John 1:1–18, and jot down anything that strikes you. Notice repeated words and themes such as "word," "life," "light," "darkness," "believe," "know," "his own," "fullness," and "breast." Yes, breast (recall our discussion in chap. 1 of this book). These are all words and themes that you will find repeated in John.

The Gospel of Abundant Life, Embodied Life, Eternal Life, Precious Life

As noted earlier, the author of this Gospel states his purpose at 20:30–31: "Now Jesus did many other signs in the presence of his disciples, which are not written in this book. But these are written so that you may come to believe that Jesus is the Messiah, the Son of God, and that through believing you may have life in his name." From the get-go (OK, so it comes at the end, but John expected you to read the Gospel from start to finish in one sitting and then immediately start over so that the line between the end and beginning is less clear than a novice reader of John might assume), John has informed you that he writes, not to add to the annals of history, but to persuade you about the identity of Jesus and to cause an encounter between you and the risen Christ through the text of the Gospel. He wants you to "believe" (*pisteuō*). The verb "believe" occurs ninety-eight times in the Gospel of John; the noun never appears. Believing is a verb, an action. Was then and is now. The author tells you at the end of chapter 21 that he left out numerous details but that he has provided all that is necessary for you to believe that Jesus is the Messiah, the Son of God, and that believing leads to life. Abundant life, embodied life, eternal life, precious life.

Creation and Genesis

The opening of John recalls the opening of Genesis. From the phrase "in [the] beginning," to the emphasis on God's Word as a creative force, to the language of light and darkness, Genesis is ever present in John—not just in the Prologue but throughout. John wants us to perceive that the stuff of earth is the stuff of God. Not a single thing that has been created was created apart from God. It all came from God, it all belongs to God, it all testifies to and reveals God. In this way, creation itself is a sacrament, a means of grace. For John, with the incarnation—God becoming flesh—bread is no longer just bread (see chap. 6), flesh is no longer just flesh, water is no longer just water (see chaps. 3, 4, 7, 19). Vines, branches, sheep, shepherds—all of them reveal the nature of God and identity of Christ.

No wonder, then, that in healing the blind man (chap. 9), Jesus takes dirt and mixes it with saliva and puts it on the man's eyes. Surely Jesus could have skipped all the messy, dirty parts and just healed the guy, as he does elsewhere (see chap. 5). But the use of the earth and the spit should remind us of the creation as told by Genesis, where God creates the first person using the earth. (God creates *adam*, the "earth creature," from the *adamah*, "earth." Notice the play on words.) John is interested in creation. He has a brief litmus test for what is Christian and what isn't: if it is life giving, if it promotes the flourishing of all creation, then it is Christian; if it is death dealing, it may be real, but it is not ultimate and is certainly not Christian: "The thief comes only to steal and kill and destroy. I came that they may have life, and have it abundantly" (10:10). Abundant life. "From his *fullness*, we have all received" (1:16).

And the Genesis creation story appears all the way to the end of the Gospel. Recall the scene in the garden, the interaction between Mary Magdalene and Jesus. The text tells us that she took him for "the Gardener." Not "a" gardener, mind you, but *the* Gardener. We remember Gardener God. This scene rectifies the fall, in effect, and brings us back to the unity shared between Adam(ah) and Eve in the original garden. The rectification is now exemplified through Jesus and Mary Magdalene.

Let me explain a bit more. In Genesis 2:7 we find that the first human person, called in Hebrew *adam*, is formed of dust from the *adamah*, "the earth." Literally, *adam* means "earth-creature"; it's not a proper name as such. It is symbolic language. Likewise, when the next human creature is made, she is named *havah*, from the Hebrew verb "to live," because she is the "mother of all living things" (Gen. 3:20). In English translations, these get put into the proper names Adam and Eve and get detached from their original beautiful, meaning-heavy roots.[1] As the story unfolds in Genesis, gender comes into existence, and it is a source of alienation.[2] In John 20 (and John 4, truth be told), alienation gives way to reconciliation and redemption.

Jesus as Lady Wisdom

John brilliantly presents Jesus in the role of Lady Wisdom in a number of ways. As we read in numerous Septuagint (LXX) texts,[3] Lady Wisdom (Heb. *hokhmah*, Gk. *sophia*) is God's partner: she helps to create the world, she delights in the human race, she continually

1. Do yourself a huge favor and read "A Love Story Gone Awry" by Phyllis Trible, in *God and the Rhetoric of Sexuality* (Philadelphia: Fortress Press, 1978), 72–143. You will never read Genesis the same way again. Never.

2. Cf. Wayne A Meeks, "The Image of the Androgyne," *History of Religions* 13, no. 3 (Feb. 1974): 165–208. In this classic article Meeks shows that the earliest Jewish thinkers consider gender categories something to be overcome. That is, the original earth-creature was integrated and whole. Gender differentiation brought alienation and hierarchy. The apostle Paul reflects the utopian vision whereby we all become androgynous when he cites the baptismal formula of Gal. 3:28: "There is no longer Jew or Greek, there is no longer slave or free, there is no longer male and female; for all of you are one in Christ Jesus."

3. LXX is shorthand for the Septuagint (Latin for seventy). This is the Greek translation of the Hebrew Scriptures, produced in Alexandria around the second century BCE. According to the tradition transmitted by the Letter of Aristeas (second-century BCE text), King Ptolemy II summoned seventy Jewish scholars to translate the Hebrew Scriptures into Greek for his library in Alexandria.

tries to help humans to get knowledge and flee from ignorance. She cries aloud incessantly. Unfortunately, the Old Testament tells us that she is often rejected, because fools hate knowledge and humans would rather wallow in ignorance, for the most part. This theme is played out mightily in John, as there is ongoing irony related to who "knows" what and what really counts as saving knowledge (the verb *oida*, "know," appears eighty-four times in John but only twenty-four times in Matthew, twenty-one in Mark, twenty-five times in Luke; the verb *ginosko*, another word for "know," appears fifty-seven times in John, twenty in Matthew, twelve in Mark, twenty-eight times in Luke). Read the Prologue alongside Proverbs 8:22–31; Sirach 24:1–9; and Proverbs 1:20–32. You will see that John casts Jesus in the mold of Lady Wisdom. Given this fact, the reader should not be surprised by the statement in John 1:11 that the Word/Wisdom/Jesus came unto his own and his own did not receive him.

Jesus as the Locus of the Divine

The NRSV says, "And the Word became flesh and lived among us" (1:14). That may be too banal. The verb there is *skēnoō*, a lively, allusive verb that means "to spread a tent."[4] John is pointing to the Old Testament texts that refer to God's presence among human beings. For John, Jesus is that locus. The rest of John fills out the implications of the incarnation. The incarnation is John's leitmotif, so maybe it could be ours as well.

Questions Raised by the Prologue

The Prologue has generated mountains of publications. In a nutshell, here's why.

First, there's the question of genre. The Prologue appears to be a hymn, written in poetic form.

4. One of my favorite books on John is Mary Coloe's *God Dwells with Us: Temple Imagery in the Gospel of John* (Wilmington, DE: Michael Glazier, 2001). She unpacks the rich, beautiful, significant background of our text. In some places it's a little bit tricky for those who don't know the Greek alphabet, but you will still get a lot of benefit from reading it.

John 1:1–5

Ἐν ἀρχῇ ἦν ὁ λόγος,	In the beginning was the Word,
καὶ ὁ λόγος ἦν πρὸς τὸν θεόν,	and the Word was with God,
καὶ θεὸς ἦν ὁ λόγος.	and the Word was God.
οὗτος ἦν ἐν ἀρχῇ πρὸς τὸν θεόν.	He was in the beginning with God.
παντα δι' αὐτοῦ ἐγένετο,	All things came into being through him
καὶ χωρὶς αὐτοῦ ἐγένετο οὐδὲ ἕν.	[and without him not one thing came into being].
ὃ γέγονεν ἐν αὐτῷ ζωὴ ἦν,	What has come into being in him was life,
καὶ ἡ ζωὴ ἦν τὸ φῶς τῶν ἀνθρώπων·	and the life was the light of all people.
καὶ τὸ φῶς ἐν τῇ σκοτίᾳ φαίνει,	The light shines in the darkness,
καὶ ἡ σκοτία αὐτὸ οὐ κατέλαβεν.	and the darkness did not overcome it.

Hymns are fairly common in the New Testament. They are mentioned in Ephesians 5:19 and Colossians 3:16. Parts of hymns appear in Philippians 2:6–11; Colossians 1:15–20; and 1 Timothy 3:16. In a famous letter exchange well worth reading between Pliny the Younger, who was governor of Pontus/Bithynia 111–13 CE, and the emperor Trajan, Pliny mentions that Christians "were accustomed to meet on a fixed day before dawn and sing responsively a hymn to Christ as to a god" (Pliny, *Letters* 10.96). Jewish hymns are quite common, as we find in the material from Qumran. But what is the original context for the hymn in John? Was it originally a Jewish hymn in honor of John the Baptist? Was it a Jewish hymn in honor of Lady Wisdom? Was it a hymn originally composed in honor of Lady Wisdom and then adopted by followers of John the Baptist and then taken over by Johannine Christians to apply to Jesus? Much speculation abounds.

The hymn has clearly been influenced by the Wisdom tradition, which includes the book of Job, Psalms, the book of Proverbs,

Ecclesiastes, and Song of Songs. The book of Wisdom (also known as Wisdom of Solomon) and Sirach (also known as Ben Sira or Ecclesiasticus) are also part of this literature, though most Protestants don't know these books. (If you have a study Bible with the apocryphal/deuterocanonical books you will find them between the Old and New Testaments.) Some Christians consider them scriptural and some do not. You have just read the Prologue in the light of Proverbs 8:22–31; Sirach 24:1–9; and Proverbs 1:20–32. You overachievers may want to take the time now to read also Psalm 33:6; Wisdom of Solomon 9:1–3; and Baruch 3:9–4:4. Notice the similarities (and differences) between the role of Lady Wisdom and the role of Jesus.

In addition to Wisdom literature, others have suggested that the Prologue has been influenced by Gnosticism, Jewish and Greek philosophy, and, of course, Genesis. Also, what is its relationship to the rest of the Gospel? Does it signal major themes that appear throughout the Gospel, or is it disconnected and rather "tacked on"? Spoiler alert: you will see that I find it to be tightly connected with the rest of the Gospel.

John the Baptist has a unique role in the Fourth Gospel. How does he figure in John, especially as compared with the Synoptics?

In fact, noticing how different the beginning of the Fourth Gospel is may make one wonder about the overall relationship between the Fourth Gospel and the Synoptic Gospels. Does John know the material in the Synoptics? If so, how does the Fourth Gospel relate? Is it a correction or a supplement?

I've included other questions to consider at the end of this chapter as you study the Prologue.

John 1:29–42: Come and See and Hear and Know and Believe and Then Testify!

The Gospel of John is a dramatic, gripping narrative. John 1:29–42 divides into two main parts: verses 29–34 and verses 35–42.

Act 1: Background

The play has already begun at 1:1, of course, with the great Prologue (1:1–18), in which John the Baptist first appears (1:6–8, 15). John the

Baptist looms large in 1:19–28. The leaders of Jerusalem interrogate John, asking after his identity. John treads the *via negativa,* which the Prologue has taught us to expect from him. The Prologue states that John was *not* the light, but was a testifier (from the Gk. *martys,* whence we derive the English word "martyr"). Likewise, John triply confesses that he is *not* the Messiah (v. 20), he is *not* Elijah (v. 21), and he is *not* "the prophet" (probably a reference to Moses' declaration in Deut. 18:15). Still, the leaders press antagonistically, demanding a statement; so John turns to Scripture and places his ministry in the context of words of the prophet Isaiah. They ask him about the meaning of his baptizing practices, and he immediately does what he does best in the Fourth Gospel: he testifies to Jesus and his preeminence, in the spirit of the words already mentioned in the Prologue at verse 15. And he makes a key observation about the inquisitors: they do not know Jesus. Here we should hear dramatic music or a gong or something of that sort, since we are supposed to recall 1:11 at this point ("He came to what was his own, and his own people did not accept him"). John the Baptist and Jesus have not yet interacted in the narrative, but we have been superbly set up for that pregnant imminent moment.

Act 2: Jesus and John the Baptist Interact (1:29–34)

The day after his run-in with the authorities, John the Baptist *sees* Jesus and *testifies* about his identity: "*See* the Lamb of God, who takes away the sin of the world." Note the following:

1. Jesus takes away the sin of the cosmos (Gk. *kosmos*), not the church, just as in 3:16 we hear that God so loved the cosmos, and in 4:42 the Samaritans recognize Jesus as the savior of the cosmos, not just the church. Jesus himself declares in 12:32: "And I, when I am lifted up from the earth [referring to his crucifixion], will draw *all people* to myself" (my italics).

2. Try not to read the atonement theology that you are familiar with, from Hebrews and perhaps Paul and certainly the Johannine Epistles, into the Gospel of John. Jesus becomes a paschal lamb of sorts in the way that *every* holy metaphor, tradition, and space dear to Judaism (and Samaritanism, for that matter) finds its fulfillment in Jesus according to the Johannine community, including the temple

(chaps. 2 and 4), Moses, Scripture (5:39ff), the manna in the wilderness (chap. 6), the various "festivals of the Judeans," Abraham (chap. 8, esp. vv. 53–59), and so on. Therefore, it is not surprising that the significance of Passover would in some way be fulfilled in Jesus for John.[5] Indeed, in the Gospel of John, Jesus is killed a day earlier than he is in the Synoptic Gospels. That is, by the time he is enjoying the Last Supper in the Synoptics, he is already dead in John. In John, he is killed on the day when the Passover lamb is sacrificed (for a helpful chart on this, go to the Johannine literature website run by New Testament scholar Felix Just (http://catholic-resources.org/Bible/Jesus-Death.htm).

But Jesus is never considered a ransom in John, nor is he a "lamb led to the slaughter," whose death was a "humiliation" (as in Acts 8:31–32). In fact, Jesus clearly and repeatedly states that he lays down his life of his own accord. He has the power to lay it down and the power to take it up again (10:17–18). No, John simply piles up metaphors on Jesus to impress upon you the significance, identity, and ultimacy of Jesus. He is simultaneously the Lamb of God and the Good Shepherd (chap. 10) who knows his sheep and who asks Peter to feed his lambs (chap. 21).

In the rest of this act, you find John the Baptist again testifying to Jesus, promoting Jesus, and demoting himself (cf. 3:30). Notice the emphatic, repetitive language. He sees (v. 32), he hears (v. 33), he moves from ignorance to knowledge (vv. 32–33) by a revelation, and then he *testifies*: "And I myself have seen and have *testified* that this is the Son of God." The whole Gospel of John was written for no other reason than to reveal Jesus to us, to provide a space for us to encounter him in his full identity. The author clearly tells you in 20:31 (probably the original ending of the Gospel): "But these are written so that you may come to believe that Jesus is the Messiah, the Son of God, and that through believing you may have life in his name."

5. The use of "fulfillment" language here may raise questions about supersessionism or "replacement theology" either at the level of the Johannine community or later Christian theological developments (which employ biblical texts). For more discussion on this, be sure to read the essay provided in the Appendix.

Act 3: Come and See (1:35–42)

The final act of John's inaugural proclamation parallels the previous day. Once again John *sees* Jesus and testifies: "*See* the Lamb of God." On the basis of *hearing the testimony* of another person, John's disciples follow Jesus. It begins with Jesus directly addressing them: "What do you seek?" (In this Gospel, Jesus always asks pointed, direct questions.) He invites them to "come and see." They hang out with Jesus (Gk. *menō*, "abide"), which leads to their deep intimate encounter with him. This results in a rich, eternal-life-giving experience of their own with Jesus, such that their faith is no longer derivative of someone else's but is now based on their own intimate relationship with Jesus.

And so goes the pattern throughout John, as you see already in verse 41. Andrew has been found by eternal life, and what does he do? He immediately testifies that Jesus is the Messiah (remember 20:31?) and invites his brother Simon to "come and see"/encounter Jesus for himself. An intimate encounter occurs, and Simon follows. In the very next passage Philip becomes a follower and immediately testifies to Nathaniel, using the same words that Jesus did: "Come and see" (1:46). The Samaritan woman does the same thing in chapter 4. She hangs out and engages Jesus deeply, his identity is revealed to her, she is flooded by eternal life, and she goes out to testify and to tell her fellow Samaritans, "Come and see." They do come and "hang out" with Jesus (v. 40), and they have a direct revelation of their own that leads them to testify: "They said to the woman, 'It is no longer because of what you said that we believe, for we have heard for ourselves, and we know that this is truly the Savior of the world'" (v. 42).

So what are we waiting for? Let's go testify for the sake of abundant, eternal life!

Questions for Reflection

Prologue

1. What are the issues of date, audience, and setting of the Gospel?
2. Read Proverbs 8. How does it relate to chapter 1?
3. How does the beginning of the Fourth Gospel differ from the beginning of the Synoptics?

4. Why all this business about John the Baptist?
5. Who are "his own"?
6. Do you feel this day as if the darkness has not overcome the light?
7. How does verse 14 strike you? Does it raise questions? What does tabernacling mean to you? "Glory" is a big John word. What does it mean to you? Do "glory," "grace," and "truth" describe the life of discipleship for you right now? Why or why not? What words would you use?
8. Do you feel that Jesus has been made known to you yet?

John 1:29–42

1. What problems do you see? What strikes you? What issues deserve further thought?
2. How does the genre influence the presentation?
3. What did the author intend to say to the listeners?
4. How does the passage further the author's agenda? How would it affect the Gospel if it were omitted?
5. How does the passage fit into the larger Gospel and its arguments, themes, and so forth?
6. How does the story relate to reality, both that of Jesus' ministry and that of John's own community some sixty years later? What about your community?

Chapter 3

Night Moves by Nicodemus

John 3

There's something for everyone in the story of Nicodemus. He is one of the most "open" characters in the story, because he can be interpreted in many different ways. Nicodemus is an unusual "minor" character because he is the only one who keeps showing up throughout the story, in three different places in John: chapters 3, 7, and 19. He appears nowhere else in the whole Bible. You might want to read each of these chapters before proceeding.

Who is Nicodemus? The text tells us three facts about him right way. First, he is a Pharisee. Many Christians make a mistake when they automatically interpret Pharisees in a negative, caricatured fashion. Unfortunately, this caricature has even entered the dictionary meaning itself; but it is not an accurate description of real Pharisees in the first century. If you look at Dictionary.com, you'll see what I mean. Definition #1 is fine; definition #2 is the culprit.

> *noun*
>
> 1. a member of a Jewish sect that flourished during the 1st century B.C. and 1st century A.D. and that differed from the Sadducees chiefly in its strict observance of religious ceremonies and practices, adherence to oral laws and traditions, and belief in an afterlife and the coming of a Messiah.
>
> 2. (lowercase) a sanctimonious, self-righteous, or hypocritical person.

In the first century there were different "flavors" of Judaism, just as there have always been different flavors of Christianity. Four of the most notable were Pharisees, Sadducees, Essenes, and Zealots (not to mention Christians themselves). Sadducees were the temple-based priestly aristocracy. Pharisees were experts in scriptural interpretation, Bible teaching, and legal adjudication. The Essenes were a sectarian group living by the Dead Sea in Qumran. The Zealots were nationalists with the political aim of driving out Rome, the occupying empire. When the destruction of the second temple took place in 70 CE, the Sadducees were no longer relevant, since there was no temple; the Zealots were squashed; the Essenes were decimated. Hence the Pharisees were the only group poised to assume leadership within Judaism. One might call them "proto-rabbis."

At that time, we have the end of Second Temple Judaism and the beginning of rabbinic Judaism. To this day the temple has never been rebuilt, and rabbinic Judaism continues. The Pharisees were concerned with the democratization of the tradition; that is, they wanted everyone, not just the priestly class, to be able to observe Torah in their homes and synagogues. Their attention was on the *am-ha-aretz*, the people of the earth, the everyday folks. Paul, of course, was a Pharisee until his dying day (Acts 23:6; Phil. 3:5). So was Nicodemus—a Pharisee, a leader of "the Jews" (see my essay on "the Jews," appendix 1 at the end of this book).[1] The conversation between Jesus and Nicodemus, then, is Jewish teacher to Jewish teacher, scholar to scholar. Much of the irony of the passage plays off of this fact.

We are also told that Nicodemus comes "by night." This is not an accidental piece of information. The Fourth Gospel uses much light/dark imagery, with light being good and dark being bad. The conversation starts out fine. Nicodemus, representing his group ("*we* know"), indicates that the signs that Jesus does are sourced from God. Remember that "signs" (*semeia*) is special Johannine language. In the Synoptic Gospels (Matthew, Mark, and Luke), Jesus does "deeds of power" (*dynameis,* which we often translate "miracles"), not signs. John never uses the word *dynameis*. What do signs do? They point to something. That is, the meaning of the act is not simply,

1. "'The Jews' in the Fourth Gospel," in *Feasting on the Gospels—John, Volume 1: A Feasting on the Word Commentary*, ed. Cynthia A. Jarvis and E. Elizabeth Johnson (Louisville, KY: Westminster John Knox Press, 2015), xi–xiv.

"Wow—check that out!" Rather, it is something deeper about who God is and who Jesus is. In fact, this Gospel is rather impatient with "signs faith." It might be OK as a baby step, but a mature Christian knows that a faith based on miracles is a shallow (and shaky) faith indeed.

Notice that Jesus does not stick out his chest and say, "Glad you noticed my powerful deed." Instead, he ignores Nicodemus's statement and tries to move to a deeper conversation by issuing the first of three double-amen sayings that appear in chapter 3. There are twenty-five of these double-amen ("very truly" in the NRSV) statements in John; no other Gospel has this feature. They introduce important proclamations. The signs point to the kingdom of God and how we participate in it. Whatever it entails, we must be born *anōthen*. This word has two meanings in Greek, "from above" and "again." Jesus means the former; Nicodemus interprets it as the latter and so is immediately confused and starts talking about being physically reborn. Jesus plows ahead, issuing another double-amen saying. Being born *anōthen* means: (1) being born from above, (2) being born of water and the Spirit, and (3) seeing/entering the kingdom of God.

When one hears this, baptism comes to mind. Jesus is talking about a life empowered by the Holy Spirit, not about fleshly birth. He is speaking in metaphor, while Nicodemus is stuck on the literal. Notice that one Greek word lies behind the English words "Spirit" and "wind" (and, for that matter, "breath"): *pneuma*. The author is doing wordplay here in verse 8, as he invites Nicodemus into the exciting, if unpredictable and surprising, life of the Spirit. If Nicodemus was lost before, he is even more lost now; so he questions Jesus, probably with a furrowed brow and some frustration or exasperation about Jesus' pedagogical skills! "How can these things be?" Nicodemus cannot seem to let go of the ordinary to make room for the extraordinary. He clings to what he already knows and wants everyone and everything to "stay in their lane," to fit it all into his preconceived categories. I can relate to that.

If Nicodemus is frustrated with Jesus, Jesus appears to return the favor as he chastises him. Nicodemus respectfully calls Jesus rabbi in verse 2, but Jesus' use of the term "teacher" with respect to Nicodemus conveys critique: "You are a 'teacher' but you don't understand?" He then proceeds to make what appear to be more enigmatic statements. Nicodemus never speaks with Jesus after verse 9.

By the end of chapter 3, it's hard to know how to react to Nicodemus and whether to sympathize with him or scoff at him. One feels like Tevye from *Fiddler on the Roof*! On the one hand, we are against him:

- We have already read 1:11, which tells us that Jesus came unto his own and his own did not receive him. Nicodemus represents Jesus' own.
- We wish that Nicodemus would ask questions that bespeak a serious ability to engage in spiritual matters, such as, "Define what you mean by 'flesh,' 'spirit,' 'kingdom of God,' 'born from above,' 'born from water and from spirit.'" Or "Why did you move from speaking about people in general, you plural, to me personally?" Instead, Nicodemus rebuffs Jesus' attempt at a personal encounter and invitation to consider his own status vis-à-vis the kingdom and steers the conversation back to a vague, general question (3:9). It seems that Nicodemus is either (a) incapable of deeper conversation, at least momentarily; (b) cynical and dismissive of Jesus' viewpoint; (c) concerned about what it might cost him to break formation with his group, given his elevated social status; or (d) some combination of the above.

On the other hand, we are for him:

- He does come to Jesus, even though he has a lot to lose in terms of status if he follows a loser.
- We the readers have been given a lot of information already (everything in chaps. 1–2) that Nicodemus has not been privy to.
- We ourselves, only three chapters into the Gospel, are not sure we know what Jesus is talking about.

Then there's the disorienting, ambiguous use of mixed-up personal pronouns. In verses 1–6, whenever Jesus says "you," he does so in the singular, addressing Nicodemus as an individual. In verse 7, it's half and half. The verse starts out by addressing Nicodemus directly but then treats Nicodemus as a representative of a larger group. Verse 11 begins with the singular, but switches to the plural later, never to return to Nicodemus as an individual. One gets the sense that Nicodemus is being used as a character to make a point. Furthermore, it's typical of John to employ a technique we call Johannine misunderstanding, whereby a character in the story misunderstands Jesus and so allows Jesus to expand upon a theme (which is to say, it allows the author of the Gospel to expand upon a theme he wants the reader to understand). The character is a kind of springboard.

If that's the case, what does the author want us to know? Well, we have already learned that we should be concerned to receive the Spirit, to enter the kingdom of God, and to achieve unity with God. This is done when we unite with Jesus, the one who is in God's bosom, the Son of Man (or the Human One—the Greek admits both). The Son of Man/Human One is the title Jesus uses when he talks about his passion, about being crucified. He makes a comparison between himself being "lifted up" on the cross and the serpent that Moses "lifted up" in the wilderness in Numbers 21. The word for "lifted up" is *hypsoō*; John is unique in presenting Jesus' crucifixion this way. Jesus' crucifixion is simultaneously an exaltation, a coronation, and an occasion of healing for all people, as Jesus says in 12:32: "And I, when I am lifted up, will draw *all* people to myself." Not some, mind you, but *all*. Indeed, John 3:16 tells us that God so loved *the cosmos* (Gk. *kosmos*; "world" is much too small a translation for this word) that God acted to save and heal and draw the cosmos to God. That's quite a scope. God manages simultaneously to be equally concerned with the entire cosmos and the particular individual (Nicodemus, you, me), whether or not the cosmos or the individual (Nicodemus, you, me) is concerned with God at any given moment.

If we were filming the scene, would we imagine Nicodemus remaining in Jesus' hearing all the way to 3:21? Or does Nicodemus fade out, with only Jesus remaining on screen? Whatever we decide, in chapter 3, Nicodemus has been put in a position of choice and, this time, does not choose well. Given another chance, he may.

He does appear again in John 7. He is not named until 7:45, but we might imagine him on stage beginning at verse 11, where "the Jews" appear. Remember, Nicodemus has a name, has power, has status, has clout. A new scene begins at 7:45, when the temple police come in without Jesus, to the chagrin of the chief priests and Pharisees, and testify to Jesus' charisma. At verse 50, Nicodemus steps forward. The reader has high hopes that Nicodemus will boldly stand up for Jesus. Nicodemus has already personally encountered Jesus, and he's "one of them," so he could be a bridge figure. He doesn't have the courage to make a statement, but he does test the waters by venturing a question: "Our law does not judge people without first giving them a hearing . . . does it?" Immediately his colleagues grow large and oppose him. And what does Nicodemus do? Ante up? Fight fire with fire? Testify? Not this time. He cowers before his colleagues, who shut him down and put him in his place by Bible thumping. There is a devastating lack of response from Nicodemus at this point; when called upon to choose between being a Judean (against Jesus) or a Galilean (for Jesus), he becomes silent. Their response is quite a non sequitur; Nicodemus appeals to the law, and his colleagues move to ad hominem attack. Nicodemus neither cries foul in this Gospel nor brings the discussion back to the law. Fear mutes him.

What are we to make of Nicodemus here? What effect does he have on us? Are we disappointed in him? Or do we identify with him? Or both and then some? As in chapter 3, John again carefully shows that Nicodemus belongs to a particular social group, and his encounter with Jesus places him in a precarious position vis-à-vis his own group. He belongs to the educated elite who make things happen. The reader can feel her stomach tighten and throat dry up as Nicodemus is put on the spot and must decide whether or not to do the reckless, if right, thing. Will he risk his social position for Jesus' sake, based on his limited knowledge of Jesus? Would we risk ours for Jesus? Do we?

Nicodemus appears for the last time in 19:38–42, where the author starts a new scene with the phrase "after these things." There is no reason to assume, however, that he is not part of the dramatic trial and crucifixion narrated in chapters 18–19. He shows up with Joseph of Arimathea at the tomb of Jesus. Joseph appears in all of the Gospel accounts, always very positively. Only John has Nicodemus accompany Joseph to the tomb. Immediately, the author reminds us that Nicodemus had come to Jesus "by night." It appears to be a continuing feature of Nicodemus that he acts in the dark. His desire to treat Jesus' body with spices has been interpreted in two ways. Negatively, the fact that he brings a hundred pounds of spices strikes one as overkill—such that it emphasizes that he does not expect Jesus to get back up. On the other hand, in a Gospel that loves excess, the abundance of spices, the lavish devotion to Jesus' dead body may be especially admirable; one only wishes that he had not waited to act until Jesus was dead. Given what Mary does in chapter 12 by anointing, the reader is even more disappointed at an opportunity lost. Nicodemus, different from Thomas who doubts, does not receive a postresurrection appearance. Joseph of Arimathea, though he was afraid, acts with some boldness (asking Pilate for Jesus' body) and is called a "disciple." Nicodemus is not explicitly named as such.

So, is Nicodemus a failure or a success when it comes to modeling solid discipleship? It's hard to say. What if that ambiguity is intentional? What if the open-endedness or lack of closure is a rhetorical technique that invites the reader to imagine the narrative time extending beyond the Gospel and directly into the reader's own life? What would we do if we were Nicodemus? What *are* we doing, as a matter of fact? Is our witness timid and halting or bold and risky? Or something in between?

What if Nicodemus is less of a problem to be solved, or a character to be resolved, than a personality to be experienced? Nicodemus shares some traits with the groups of which he is a part; yet he is not identical to them, even standing over against them at times. He is an individual with traits. Granting Nicodemus a proper name constructs him as a personage in a clearer, stronger way. The fact that he appears named three times strengthens that experience.

It seems that there is something about Nicodemus's social, religious, political status that makes it hard for him to cross over. Nicodemus then might be read differently by readers of different social locations. Perhaps the poor, marginalized reader would identify with the Samaritan woman or the blind man and take a certain glee in this educated, high-status character not "getting it." But the educated, high-status reader with much to lose in terms of social standing by following Jesus might find the character of Nicodemus true to her own situation. I find the various, opposing reactions to Nicodemus among readers, scholarly or otherwise, fascinating.

Nicodemus should be considered a major character, since he punctuates the Gospel regularly. If the reader easily discerns that she should follow characters who represent the Gospel's values (believing, publicly testifying on behalf of Jesus and inviting others to encounter Jesus, loving, transforming) and avoid thinking and behaving like the characters who represent that which the narrator rejects (denial, betrayal, fear), then Nicodemus should not be considered a representative figure. Rather, he may be the character with whom the reader most identifies since he conveys potential. The reader wants Nicodemus to make the right choice, to identify himself with Jesus, but she also understands that he has much more to lose than others might. He is a complex character with high social status. The reader turns him round and round like a prism, seeing the different angles, and, in doing so, catches perhaps a glimpse of the complexity of her own motives and the potential cost of following Jesus.

No character resists closure more than Nicodemus. Most characters are tidily dealt with and are models for good or ill. Even Peter, who denies Jesus, gets rehabilitated by the end. Nicodemus, on the other hand, functions in the Fourth Gospel much as the women function in Mark 16:8. It is the very *lack* of closure that grips the reader and makes her, finally, "mind the gap" between Nicodemus and closure. She will, God willing, assume the role of Nicodemus and walk through the resurrection appearances in chapters 19–21, deciding finally to commit to the risen Son of God in the way she/Nicodemus could not or would not commit to the preresurrected Jesus. In that way, she may finally move from having her mind on earthly things (power, status, fear, shame) to heavenly things (Christ, God, birth from above). Jesus asks Nicodemus, "How can you understand heavenly things if you do not understand earthly things?" The answer is the narrative of Fourth Gospel. Nicodemus (and the reader) needs the whole story, through chapter 21, to understand—much as the disciples need the whole story to understand, as the narrator indicates in 2:22.

To the rest of that story we now turn. Well, almost.

Contesting the Light/Dark Dualism

I want to address directly a complicated issue—the association of *light* with hope and goodness, and *dark* with pain and evil. It's an age-old metaphor and clearly useful, on the one hand. Our Scriptures and hymns are full of such language, some more welcome than others. Take, for example, "Grace That Is Greater," a beautiful hymn that I love to sing. One stanza goes like this:

> Dark is the stain that we cannot hide;
> What can avail to wash it away?
> Look! There is flowing a crimson tide,
> Whiter than snow you may be today.

Perhaps the lyricist is referring to Revelation 7:14 ("Then he said to me, 'These are they who have come out of the great ordeal; they have washed their robes and made them white in the blood of the Lamb'"), though the hymnal I have open at present to quote these lyrics does not indicate that it refers to Revelation (instead, it quotes Rom. 5:21).[2] And the hymn doesn't say your robe may be white; it says you may be white. So does "Nothing but the Blood."

James Weldon Johnson's lyrics in "Lift Every Voice" also rely upon metaphors of darkness and light:

> Sing a song full of the faith that the dark past has taught us.
> Sing a song full of the hope that the present has brought us.
> Facing the rising sun of our new day begun . . .[3]

In his chapter on the Gospel of John, in the excellent resource *True to Our Native Land: An African American New Testament Commentary*, Allen Dwight Callahan interprets some of the stunning paintings associated with the Gospel of John done by the famous African American artist Henry Ossawa Tanner. Addressing Tanner's "Nicodemus Visiting Christ" painting, Callahan writes: "The highlights of Jesus' face shine as he speaks and gestures in near-darkness; illumination at the same time emanates in and transcends thought and language, thought's human sound. As Jesus speaks, the light of the world enters the darkness of Nicodemus' ignorance."[4] The dualities of black and white, dark and light, can serve as useful metaphors indeed and have proved capable of expanding to incorporate additional layers of meaning. For example, in the Callahan

2. *Worship His Majesty* (Alexandria, IN: Gaither Music Co., 1987), hymn 482.

3. *The United Methodist Hymnal Book of United Methodist Worship* (Nashville: The United Methodist Publishing House, 1989), hymn 519.

4. Allen Dwight Callahan, "John," in *True to our Native Land: An African American New Testament Commentary* (Minneapolis: Fortress Press, 2007), 189.

quote above, we see darkness pointing toward ignorance. Associating negative traits with darkness and positive ones with lightness allows for a visualization of abstract characterizations in literary and artistic portrayals.

But here's the problem as I see it at the moment: associating light with white and darkness with black/brown leads to danger in the real world, where these dualisms get mapped onto real people's bodies. Thanks to womanist and postcolonial scholars, among others, there is no longer any denying that these dualistic schemas can promote the valuing of some bodies (white), while patently devaluing the bodies of others (not white) by those in power (who have, historically, been disproportionately white).

Lest you think I live in an ivory tower and am enslaved by political correctness (I am a white American female, by the way), "the doll tests"—Google it for yourself—have found this to be true, decade after decade, test after test. Little girls of color will almost always prefer the white doll:

> At one point, the interviewer asked one girl to pick which doll was the nicest, to which the girl responded by picking up the white doll—but when asked which was the bad doll, she picked the black one. When the interviewer asked her why she chose the "bad" doll the way she did, the girl had a surprising answer: "It's black."[5]

To anyone who's been paying attention or is old enough, it's actually not surprising at all. The test was first performed in the 1940s.

I say the issue is complicated because, as a white person, I do not deign to tell people of color (especially James Weldon Johnson!) to stop using particular metaphors that are meaningful to them as individuals or communities. In fact, I do not deign to limit for *anyone* of *any* color the power of a particular metaphor. I do aim, however, to remind all of us that language has power and that we should use it carefully, always weighing the promises and the pitfalls of our choices. If we find that a metaphor dear to us (especially those of us who enjoy the most power) is causing injury to another (especially to those of us who have the least power), can we let go of it and make space for one that gives life to a broader number of our brothers and

5. http://lybio.net/tag/doll-test-quotes; accessed October 18, 2016.

sisters? As the great philosopher of language Ludwig Wittgenstein declared: "The limits of my language mean the limits of my world." We may have *good* language for the moment, but we should always be grasping for *better* language. In this case, the voice of the person with the least power should matter the *most.* Is it not incumbent upon the person in the majority—whatever that may be, with respect to power, race, gender, ethnicity, sexual orientation, ability, class, and so forth—to adopt a position of openness to their wisdom and experience?

Seeing Nicodemus (and Ourselves) in a Different Light

I have read with appreciation most of the New Testament scholarship on Nicodemus. But the person who has pushed me the most is my student Beth Taylor, who is a life coach. From her very first semester of seminary in my intro class, she became a champion of Nicodemus; it carried over, not surprisingly, into the seminar on John, where she did both her research paper and her creative project on Nicodemus. She has spent considerable time wrestling with the Nicodemus passages and challenging me (and others) to see him sympathetically, as a person who overcomes the dualism of either/or, insider/outsider, and so on and, instead, models the path of Christian discipleship that honors being and becoming. Here are some of her excellent points and questions:

- Numerous characters in John show movement in their faith as they engage Jesus more fully (consider the Samaritan woman in chap. 4, Martha of Bethany in chap. 11, and Mary Magdalene in chap. 20). While they accomplish this within one passage, Nicodemus's progress develops more gradually across the narrative.
- Taylor sees the three episodes as paralleling three aspects of our faith journeys: our personal lives (Nicodemus's private encounter with Jesus in chap. 3); our public witness (Nicodemus with his compatriots in chap. 7); and our involvement in Christian community (as he joins Joseph of Arimathea and perhaps other Christians [including Mary Magdalene] at the tomb).
- The image of light itself lends itself far more to a spectrum than an either/or dualism.

Duality presents an either/or choice. A life of faith includes long stretches of gray that lie between complete darkness and the full knowledge of God. Jesus moves each person forward on that continuum in each conversation he has with them. What matters is whether the character moves toward or away from the light of relationship with Jesus. For this reason, the absoluteness of the dark/light metaphor breaks down when one actually considers the nature of light and darkness, whether physically, cosmologically, or in terms of faith development. Physically, there are gradients of light. The eye adjusts gradually to changes in the amount of light available. As people grow accustomed to the level of light available, it becomes the comfortable state in which to live. Cosmologically, no one remains in complete darkness, because the light is present in the world. It is also clear that the Fourth Evangelist acknowledges that no one's faith development remains static. The Gospel highlights the tension between the darkness that pulls people away from belief and the light that draws people into relationship. Development of relationship is a process that moves a person toward deeper faith. One becomes a child of God through a process of growth that is generated by being in contact with Jesus.[6]

Taylor invites us into a meditation that involves props. A lamp represents Jesus and the power to which we have access when we are plugged into Jesus, the Holy Spirit, and the Christian community. Just as the lamp is plugged into the source of power flowing through the entire city, Jesus is intimately connected with God the Father and God the Spirit. Taylor reminds us that the same power by which Jesus is resurrected is available to us when we are connected with Jesus.

Light bulbs represent each of us as we were created with our various gifts and traits. Taylor then asks each of us to identify at least ten traits we possess by nature and write those on a bulb. For example, she sees Nicodemus as intelligent, tenacious (to have reached his status), dedicated, inquisitive, and cautious; he is a good listener who is passionate in a quiet way. She says, "This bulb represents Nicodemus. It's a good bulb, well formed, and perfectly designed for its

6. Beth Taylor, "Movement toward the Light: Nicodemus and Becoming a Child of God" (unpublished paper, Perkins School of Theology, December 5, 2014).

niche in life. It is also uniquely designed, just as each person is the unique handiwork of God. Nicodemus has a lot going for him, but he is not plugged into Jesus—yet. He is meant to come alive so that he produces what he was created to produce. He was meant to share his gifts with those around him."

Many of us are less aware than Nicodemus of our desire for connection with the light, because we are comfortable, secure in our status in the community, our reputations, or our perceived value apart from God. However as illuminating those things might be, they are dim when compared to the light that shines when the Spirit flows through our filament and out into the world.

She then screws the bulb representing Nicodemus into the lamp. The direction that causes the bulb to light up is toward Jesus, the Holy Spirit, and the community. When connected, the bulb fulfills its purpose. When you unscrew the bulb, cutting off those sources of light, the bulb does not shine; it falls short of its purpose.

Taylor then invites all of us to screw our bulbs into the multibulb candelabra. As each individual turns their bulb toward connection with Jesus, they join in the flow of the Spirit, and together the community shines brilliantly in the world. Encounter with Jesus continually deepens our relationship and brightens the light shining into the world through us.

What would it take for you to plug (back) in, to turn (back) toward deeper connection with the light? How would the world be gifted if you did? What would this look like at the level of your church within the larger community?

Nicodemus came out of the darkness into the Light when he spoke with Jesus in chapter 3. Did he carry a glimmer with him when he left Jesus' presence? He felt a flicker of identification with Jesus in chapter 7 but backed away under pressure. In chapter 19, he participated in a deeply intimate act. Did he shine for only that moment, or did he remain connected and continue to deepen his relationship with Jesus through involvement in the community? What about you? Will you turn your bulb toward or away from deeper connection with the Source of Power and Light?

Chapter 4

The Gospel Wouldn't Work without Her: The Samaritan Woman

John 4

*I*f this story were ever removed from John, I would cease to be a Johannine scholar. As I write this, an icon from the church located at Jacob's well (in modern Nablus, ancient Shechem) sits on my desk, as does the (surely?) authentic oil lamp from nearby that I bought. How I came to own the icon is a story of one of my most profound experiences of walking on holy ground (a story with many layers from antiquity down to this very minute, which involves saints of old, the priest who serves the current community in the West Bank, and current soul friends who were on the trip with me; it's a story that I will always treasure).

The icon, the oil lamp, and even the pair of earrings that I wear (made from Roman glass found in the area near the well) are, I think, all attempts on my part to honor and connect with this sister from long ago whose testimony continues to change lives even now. If you want one story from this Gospel that serves as a microcosm, this is it. The Gospel wouldn't work without her. So let's dive into this story of living water, ask questions, and press God for a revelation.

But first, an important lesson, learned the hard way.

Don't Confuse John 4 with 1 John 4!

Years ago, my friend who's a Baptist pastor agreed to do a wedding in his church for two Catholics who lived in the town. Like many of us, the couple had a complicated situation. Both had been married before and had children. They were living together with a blended family. Due to the divorces and the living together, and so on, the local Catholic priest would not marry them, so they asked my friend. He agreed but of course required the typical premarital counseling. Along the way, something came up so that he wasn't going to be able to perform the ceremony itself. As a professional courtesy, I agreed to step in for that day. I met the couple only one time before the night of the rehearsal.

At the rehearsal we were running through the service. First John 4, especially verses 16–19, is a regular favorite for weddings, as it should be:

> So we have known and believe the love that God has for us. God is love, and those who abide in love abide in God, and God abides in them. Love has been perfected among us in this: that we may have boldness on the day of judgment, because as he is, so are we in this world. There is no fear in love, but perfect love casts out fear; for fear has to do with punishment, and whoever fears has not reached perfection in love. We love because he first loved us.

Perfect wedding material.

It was time for the Scripture reader to come up and practice the reading. From the pew, she held up a paper showing me that she was "on it" and definitely prepared and had already printed out the text. I was being pressured to hurry up because they had reservations for the rehearsal dinner at a restaurant. Also, it was awkward because I didn't really know them, so I didn't want to be difficult. So we skipped the practice reading.

The next day at the wedding, with cameras rolling, the reader stands up and reads not 1 John 4 but *John* 4! Verses 16–19 of *John* 4 read as follows:

> [Jesus] said to her, "Go, call your husband, and come back." The woman answered him, "I have no husband." Jesus said to her, "You are right in saying, 'I have no husband'; for you have had five husbands, and the one you have now is not your husband. What you have said is true!" The woman said to him, "Sir, I see that you are a prophet."

Obviously, I knew from the first word out of her mouth where this was going. But I didn't know them well, the cameras were rolling, and I had to make a split-second decision. In that moment I said to God, "OK, here's what I know for sure—you exist and, for some reason, you hate me! I'm going to assume that *someone* here (certainly not *me*) needs to hear John 4 instead of 1 John 4!" No one seemed to notice; certainly no one mentioned it. I'm usually sad when people don't know their Bible well; that day, I was sort of grateful.

Now hear this: I know that 1 John is a little book that can be hard to find, but please know that John and 1 John are not the same! Also, know that if you ever ask me to perform your wedding, I will insist that the Scripture reading be practiced in my hearing at the rehearsal, no matter how late your party is to your reserved dinner.

Attention to Detail

As you can see, details are important. So break out your Bible and read the passage, 4:1–30. I also highly recommend watching the clip from the *Gospel of John* movie that goes with the passage (Disc 1, Scene 5, Jesus and the Samaritan Woman). John starts the story by telling us that Jesus has to go through Samaria. Maybe so, but he sure as heck doesn't have to *stop* there, and, in fact, it's noteworthy that he did. The animosity between Jews and Samaritans was thick. Think of a neighborhood where you don't belong and where you'd stand out in a way that would get you at least heckled. Jesus chooses to go to Samaria for theological and personal reasons.[1] He goes to prove that he is the Savior of the whole world, including Samaritans, and he goes because that's where the Samaritan woman who needs him is.

From the outset, allow me this disclaimer: due to the brilliant way that John has crafted this story, bringing together the political/national, the religious, and the personal, it is nearly impossible to keep the threads separate when trying to present the main points in an introductory perusal. I will try to speak to the different trajectories, but they will inevitably mix.

1. In going from Judea to Galilee, normally one would have proceeded down the Jordan Rift Valley, thus skirting Samaria on the eastern side, or down the coastal highway, thus skirting it on the western side. Both would be faster than the hilly and mountainous route through the interior of Samaria, where Sychar / Shechem is.

Jesus plops down at Jacob's well. It's high noon, bright light of day. Remember the Prologue? "The true light, which enlightens everyone, was coming into the world." The world includes *everyone*, even Samaritans. Up walks the Samaritan woman. Recall chapter 3, where Jesus interacts with Nicodemus, who came to Jesus by night. In contrast, the Samaritan woman meets the light of the world at the brightest time of the day, so she is to be commended according to John, who told us in 3:19–21: "And this is the judgment, that the light has come into the world, and people loved darkness rather than light because their deeds were evil. For all who do evil hate the light and do not come to the light, so that their deeds may not be exposed. But those who do what is true come to the light, so that it may be clearly seen that their deeds have been done in God."

I find that many people link the fact of noon with this woman being (ironically) a "lady of the evening," or some such. The text does not say that. The woman had husbands, not customers. Rather, Nicodemus is a foil for the Samaritan woman in the same way that Judas will be for Mary of Bethany.

It's not just the time of day that drips with meaning but also the location—Jacob's well. Jacob, her ancestor, wrestled with God at another body of water. And what else happens at wells in the Old Testament? They are betrothal sites. Rebekah, Isaac's future wife, is found at a well (Gen. 24:10–61); Jacob meets Rachel at a well (Gen. 29:1–20); Moses' marriage to Zipporah is tied to a well (Exod. 2:16–22).[2] We have already seen Jesus in action at a wedding (chap. 2) and heard John declare him to be the bridegroom in 3:29.

She's going about her business, and now Jesus demands that she give him a drink. "Get a life," she says. Or in other words, "How is it that you, a Jewish male, ask me, a Samaritan woman, for a drink?" For Jesus and this Samaritan woman to relate, by definition, involves the crossing of deeply established ethnic and gender boundaries. Jesus pushes forcefully across the boundaries in order to give life. Do we? In effect, he says, "Get a life." Or better, "Receive the life I'm giving."

2. Sandra Schneiders's chapter on the Samaritan woman, "Inclusive Discipleship," in her book, *Written That You May Believe* (New York: Crossroad, 2003), has deeply influenced my views. Her scholarship is impeccable, and she is a luminary in the field of Johannine studies.

Now this lady wasn't born yesterday. She lives in a world where men have almost all the power and women next to none. Physical power, financial power, religious power, political power. She also knows her Scriptures better than any other character in the Gospel of John, apart from Jesus; so she knows that wells are the places where future grooms and brides meet. She does not yet know what we know about Jesus as the bridegroom. All she knows is that she's alone, unprotected, and with a foreign man who is breaking established social boundaries. She's on guard, but he doesn't appear to pose a major threat.

In this exchange, we see her tired out by life, going through the motions of survival. He offers her the water of life, and we the reader immediately think of Jesus' failed conversation with Nicodemus a chapter earlier about birth and wombs, and as Christians we think of baptism. Honestly, if we've worked with children or youth, we may burst into singing "I've Got a River of Life" at this point. When I teach this in person, those who know it sing it together and get really animated at the chorus:

> Spring up, O well (goosh, goosh, goosh, goosh) within my soul
> Spring up, O well (splish splash) and make me who-o-ole
> Spring up, O well (*tidal wave!*) and give to me-ee
> That life abundantly[3]

For her part, I doubt she's singing; if so, it may be a dirge. She's not been living; she's just been surviving, and barely doing that. Her cynicism is on display.

The Samaritan Woman as Samaria Itself

Now Jesus, this complete stranger, digs deeper into her life and asks about her husband. This provokes a deep theological conversation about proper worship and the coming Messiah. Now why would a conversation about this woman's husbands lead to such a conversation? You have to know a bit about Samaria's history to get this.[4]

You will want to refer to 2 Kings 17:13–34—a lively passage.

3. L. Casebolt, "I've Got a River of Life," http://www.hymnlyrics.org/requests/ive_got_a_river_of_life.php.

4. Schneiders, *Written That You May Believe*, 139–41.

There you will see that, from a Jewish perspective (that is, Jesus' perspective), Samaria had wedded itself to false gods after the return from Assyrian captivity: "So they worshiped the LORD but also served their own gods, after the manner of the nations from among whom they had been carried away. To this day they continue to practice their former customs. They do not worship the LORD and they do not follow the statutes or the ordinances or the law or the commandment that the LORD commanded the children of Jacob, whom he named Israel."

So, from Jesus' Jewish perspective, "Samaria's Yahwism was tainted by false worship and therefore even the "husband" she now has (a reference to her relationship with the God of the covenant) was not really her husband (see v. 18) in the full integrity of the covenantal relationship."[5]

Samaria (which the woman represents) has had five husbands (the false gods of the foreign tribes) and is in a not-quite relationship with the sixth. Jesus, the true bridegroom, makes seven, which is, of course a biblical number for completion, perfection, wholeness, peace, and *life*.

What you really have is at least two different streams of sexual imagery in the mix. On the one hand, any language of critique that is associated with sex in the passage is tied to the typical critique of all prophets when they yell at us about whoring after idols instead of committing to the God of Israel. Think of Hosea and Gomer. Highly problematic, sexist metaphors, to be sure, but readily available to our biblical authors in their own time. Let's call that the negative use of sexual metaphor.

But the Bible (and this passage) is also full of beautiful sexual metaphors and the exchange of sexual energy as well. That's the language of desire,[6] the language of betrothal, the language of togetherness.

Since she knows her prophets, she understands that Jesus the Jew is critiquing Samaritan religious practices in a typical way. That's what prophets do—yell about false worship and justice issues. That's

5. Schneiders, *Written That You May Believe*, 140.

6. For those who want an "advanced" read on the text that I find provocative and stimulating, see the section entitled "The Hydraulics of a Liquid Metaphor," in Stephen D. Moore, *Post-structuralism and the New Testament* (Minneapolis: Fortress Press, 1994), 52–54.

exactly why she moves from calling Jesus just a Jewish man to calling him a prophet. Not because he's a palm reader who can miraculously recount her crazy sexual escapades or predict the future à la the Nostradamus of the moment, but because prophets are usually in the business of reorienting us to proper worship and devotion to God (away from our various idols). Proper worship. American Protestants will be familiar with this battleground. Contemporary worship? Blended worship? Traditional worship? In a traditional building with a steeple? The local pub? A strip mall? Samaritans revered Mount Gerizim, Jews Mount Zion. Same stuff, different century. We agree that ultimately we are to worship God in spirit and truth. But we keep fighting about the details.

From debate about proper worship, they turn to the subject of Christology, the nature of the Messiah. You see, the Samaritan woman is a robust, confident, reflective theologian who engages Jesus in deeper conversation. He makes cryptic statements to her, as he did to Nicodemus (e.g., 4:10), but unlike Nicodemus, she debates and asks questions. She's intellectually and theologically curious. At that moment, Jesus reveals himself for the first time in the entire Gospel as the great "I am." The Samaritan woman receives a theophany (vision of God). Let me explain.

One of John's most famous characteristic features is the use of "I am" statements. There are two types of "I am" statements in John. The first are those where Jesus says "I am" followed by a predicate nominative. So we hear "I am the bread of life" (6:35, 48), "I am the light of the world" (8:12), "I am the gate of the sheep" (10:7, 9), "I am the good shepherd" (10:11, 14), "I am the resurrection and the life" (11:25), "I am the way and the truth and the life" (14:6), and "I am the true vine" (15:1, 5). At times these "I am" statements are bound to a particular sign performed by Jesus, as we'll see later.

But crucial to the issue of Christology and the understanding of why people consider John's Gospel to have such a high Christology is the second category of "I am" statements, those that echo God's self-designation in the Old Testament. "I am" is a divine revelatory phrase. In Exodus 3:13–22 Moses wants to know what he's supposed to say if the Israelites ask for the name of the God who sent him. God replies: "I AM WHO I AM. . . . Thus you shall say to the Israelites, I AM has sent me to you." In John 8:39–59 Jesus is wrangling with the

Jews about who belongs to which father. "The Jews" claim that their father is Abraham, to which Jesus harshly replies that, in fact, their father is the devil, who is a murderer and a liar.[7] And what's more, Jesus says: "Very truly, I tell you, before Abraham was, I am." To those versed in the Old Testament, this is a clear case of Jesus revealing his divine status. For the duller reader, John certifies this by saying, "So they picked up stones to throw at him," indicating that they interpreted this as blasphemy. The supreme revelation of Christ's identity will come with his death or exaltation or glorification: "When you lift up the Son of Man, then you will know that I am" (8:28, my trans.).

Clearly the Samaritan woman knows her Bible enough to understand that she has just had a theophany. And what does she do right away? Two things. She leaves her water jar, and she runs to testify to her larger community.

She Leaves Her Water Jar

John doesn't include pointless details, I assure you; so we should ponder this crucial detail. Why does she leave the water jar? It's a sign that she has received the living water that Jesus offers. She trades what is good for what is better. She trades survival and sustenance for abundant life. What if we left behind our water jars—which, truth be told, really never held all that much water anyway—and instead let the living waters wash over us like a blessing, refreshing, cleansing, softening? Really. Think about it. What's your water jar? What is it you're holding on to that you think is providing you security but is really enslaving you and keeping you from receiving something more important, something better, something living?

The woman at the well lets go and receives life itself back again.

7. Not surprisingly, this statement has proved problematic for Jewish-Christian relations over the years. Be sure to read the essay in the Appendix of this book where I expand and expound upon this thorny issue. It is ethically imperative for Christians to avoid anti-Semitism and anti-Judaism. The fact that some of our interpretations only unintentionally propagate these evils does not excuse us; thus, it is important for us to analyze our interpretations from this angle. For more help on this, see both Marilyn Salmon, *Preaching without Contempt: Overcoming Unintended Anti-Judaism* (Minneapolis: Fortress Press, 2006) and Amy-Jill Levine, *The Misunderstood Jew: The Church and the Scandal of the Jewish Jesus* (New York: HarperOne, 2007).

Only then does she realize she has traded living for merely surviving. And while she grips tightly to her means of survival, that water jar, she has nothing to share. The minute she understands who she truly is in relationship to Jesus, the minute Jesus washes away the pride and shame, the hurt, the defeated, defensive stance toward life that comes from her experience, she becomes full of life—abundant life, embodied life, eternal life, precious life. And what's the first thing that happens? She opens herself up to others so that she becomes a blessing to them! This woman goes from being hopelessly pragmatic to being a missionary for the good news of the abundant *life* that God gives and gives again, and gives yet again.

What is your water jar? What do you depend on instead of Jesus? What do you need for security? What are you clutching? Do you realize you're hanging on to it, but it's actually got you in its grip?

She Connects and Shares the Story of God Showing Up in Her Life

Jesus grants the Samaritan woman abundant life, and instead of even imagining hoarding it, she immediately shares the news. She "gets a life" and she shares it. But she isn't content for her people to have a secondhand faith. She insists, "Come and see!" She wants them to experience Jesus firsthand. Her story is not their story. Their deepest need at the moment is not the same as hers. But she knows for a fact that Jesus can meet them in their particular place of forgetfulness or hopelessness and breathe new life into them—abundant, eternal life. And they are grateful to this missionary, proclaimer of good news who encourages them to encounter Jesus for themselves. She understands the words of 3:30, so she doesn't make her testimony a show all about her in the starring role. Her witness multiplies when her compatriots become followers as well, proclaiming Jesus to be the Savior of the world (*cosmos*; cf. 3:16). She moves from seeing Jesus as a mere person, to seeing him as a prophet, to seeing him as the Messiah. This is a pattern you will see with another unnamed, "no-count" hero of the faith in John 9.

The Samaritan Woman Compared to Nicodemus and the Disciples

Another pattern I flagged in chapter 1 is intercharacterization, juxtaposing characters to make a point—or, in John's case, multiple points. We've seen some of the ways the Samaritan woman compares to Nicodemus. She's a person on the margins with respect to religion, ethnicity, gender, class, status, education, financial stability, and so on. Nicodemus is quite the opposite. She is "other" with respect to Jesus; Nicodemus, as a Jewish teacher of Israel, is one of Jesus' own. Nicodemus is associated with the dark, she with the light. He clams up; she has the most extended conversation with Jesus in the New Testament, receives a theophany, and progressively verbalizes her deepening understanding of his identity. And so on.

But notice how John also interlaces the Samaritan woman and the disciples. Right in the middle of the conversation about drinking, the author inserts this parenthetical note: "(His disciples had gone to the city to buy food.)" (4:8). "OK," you the reader may say. They show up back on the scene during Jesus' revelatory interaction with her. Awkward. Even more awkward is their response, or lack of. In the midst of this glorious, life-changing event, they take the tried-and-true, entirely unimaginative tack and worry about Jesus' inappropriate boundary crossing when it comes to gender. Perhaps Jesus didn't know that there was supposed to be a glass ceiling when it comes to divine revelations and commission to do ministry in the name of Jesus Christ by addressing males in the public square? Not only are they reflexively status quo here, but they are also too cowardly to own their bias. That can happen.

The Samaritan woman doesn't have time to stay and deal with their sexist notions; she has too much preaching to do to those in need of some good news. She is so effective in her testimony, the people head back to find Jesus for themselves. Meanwhile, the disciples, just like Nicodemus, are so focused on the literal level that they cannot or will not engage the spiritual significance of what lies right before them. As a result, while she is working, they are kerfuffling around. What she has sown, they will reap. She's building a foundation that they will, eventually, add to (4:37–38).

Does it strike you as surprising, unexpected, even ironic that, in contrast to Nicodemus and the disciples, this unnamed, non-Israelite, unorthodox female who finds herself passed from male to male in a society where males rule is the very one God lifts up as the example we are to follow in our faith journey? Does God still do that today?

The Samaritan Woman Personally

The Samaritan woman is a symbol for Jewish-Samaritan relations and the scope of Jesus' ministry (the cosmos; 4:42). But she also represents what happens when Jesus seeks out individuals for encounter. Many people can relate to this aspect of the story in a deep way with respect to their own lives. Jesus gets her attention by showing that he knows her intimately. He knows what she's been through. We are never told what has happened to her husbands. Jewish law stated that if one husband died childless the next brother was to marry his brother's wife (Deut. 25:5–6). This served two functions: the first-born child would be the heir to the first husband and though she could not inherit money or property, the woman would continue to have access to the provisions of the family. At any rate, Jesus knows her life has not turned out the way she has hoped or planned. Her younger self never would have imagined her older self ending up where it has, haggard and unexpectant.

This is the part of the story that really catches my attention this time around and makes me ask important questions about my own life and yours:

- Which relationships in her life most define her in the moments before and after her encounter with Jesus?
- Which relationships in your life most define you?
- How would you describe this woman?
- How would you describe yourself?
- How do you think Jesus saw this woman?
- How do you think Jesus sees you?
- What is this woman's deepest longing? What makes her heart sing? What is her passion? Does she even know? Did she used to know?

- What's your deepest longing? What makes your heart sing? What's your passion? Do you even know? Did you used to know?

This woman looks into Jesus' eyes and she sees that he knows her and loves her and is, in fact, able to deliver on his promise to give life. At that moment she needs water; so he speaks in terms of giving her living water. At the end of John, the disciples need fish; so Jesus provides fish in their nets and cooks them a meal of fish on the beach. The point isn't that Jesus is in the business of giving us water or fish; Jesus gives us whatever we most need in order to have life, literally and metaphorically. Most of us long to be truly known and loved in all our particularity, all our grime and glory, stunning successes and devastating failures. We want to know that we don't have to have perfect lives to be perfectly loved. That's the very way Jesus loves us.

> ***Prayer:*** *I never met the Samaritan woman, but I thank you, God, for her faith, for her passion to share the gospel, so that even now her faith continues to inspire faith in others. Like the Samaritan woman, may we be transformed often by Jesus Christ, so that we cannot help but proclaim that he is, indeed, the Savior not only of Jews, not only of Samaritans, but of the whole world/cosmos. Amen.*

Questions for Reflection

1. Watch one or more of the following videos: "Jesus and the Samaritan Woman" scene in *The Gospel of John* movie (Disc 1); Woman at the Well," a spoken word video by Erin Moon found on YouTube: https://www.youtube.com/watch?v=GcXoqNeDKhI; "Woman at the Well" in Dallas video, directed, edited and filmed by Reidland Tucker, https://www.youtube.com/watch?v=5y2GlmTxpkM.

   a. How do these depictions compare to what you've always assumed or heard about her?

b. How do these depictions compare to what you've learned in this chapter?
c. What do you find relevant or alien to your own experience in this time and place?

4. What questions does the story raise for you?
5. What are the challenges of identity: Who is she?
6. What relationships define her? What relationships define you?
7. Do you know this woman? Are you this woman? How do you relate to her, or not?
8. Is this period in your spiritual life a dry one? Or are springs of living water welling up and overflowing? Somewhere in between?
9. What is Jesus calling you to do?
10. What would the equivalent be for you today of a "Samaritan"? Whom would you find it hard to envision as an "insider"?

Chapter 5

Sight and Insight

John 9

*L*ike the Samaritan woman in chapter 4, the man born with a visual impairment in chapter 9 is one of the characters we are supposed to emulate. John's Gospel really lends itself to dramatic presentation, so let's divide this narrative into scenes.[1]

Scene 1: The Cure (9:1–7)

"As he walked along, he saw a man blind from birth." Unlike the man in chapter 5, this man is born with an impairment. Immediately, Jesus' disciples make the mistake of connecting suffering or disability with sin or wrongdoing (or at least questionable choices) when they ask, "Rabbi, who sinned, this man or his parents, that he was born blind?" But Jesus, in no uncertain terms, promptly and emphatically corrects them: "Neither this man nor his parents sinned." In other words, we should not assume a connection between sin and suffering. Their question is a bad question—useless at best and harmful at worst.

Too many people have been told that their suffering or that of someone close to them is their fault. Once when I was teaching this

1. Why, in this instance, am I going out of narrative order by treating John 9 here? There are a number of reasons. First, chaps. 4 and 9 go well together because both the Samaritan woman and the man born blind exemplify Johannine ideals of discipleship; so I want the reader to see the similarities between the two stories. Second, because there is a tendency among modern readers to equate sin and suffering, it is important to witness this encounter before treating chap. 5, lest the modern reader fall into the same trap the disciples themselves fell into.

passage, there was a woman present whose daughter has Down syndrome. She came up to me after the session and said, "So you're saying that it's not my fault that my daughter has Down syndrome?" I said to her, "I'm not saying it—Jesus is; but I agree with Jesus." Many people had made her feel guilty because she had her child later in life. I want to make two points here. First, we need to stop repeating stupid stuff about sin and suffering. Not all suffering has the same source, quality, quantity, degree, or "solution." Second, by sharing this story I do not mean to imply that Down syndrome is a "problem" or that suffering is even a part of the equation when it comes to Down syndrome. The suffering in this instance came from stigmatization and a theology that blames and shames.

After Jesus attacks the blame game, he makes another startling statement that is lost in most English translations. The NRSV says this: "He was born blind so that God's works might be revealed in him. We must work the works of him who sent me while it is day; night is coming when no one can work." This translation raises serious questions about God. Did God cause the man to be born with an impairment for the sole purpose of using him as a prop in a divine magic show? Does the God who sent Jesus into the world that he loved so much in order to give people abundant life cause congenital blindness, so that he might show off by curing the problem God caused? If so, why does God choose to cure some congenital impairments and not others? There is never an indication in this story that faith is a prerequisite for a cure. In fact, there is no indication at all that the man was seeking a cure.

The idea that God *causes* tragic situations raises serious questions about God's ethical character. I once had a person in a class who shared that twins were born to him. One twin died. Christian friends tried to comfort him with various reasons that God did this, from the idea that the death would drive him to God more, to an opportunity to show valiant faith and testify in the midst of tragedy. He did not find help in any of these scenarios in which God killed his child, and I can see why. To say that God can *redeem* a tragic situation is quite different from saying that God *causes* tragic situations.

Two comments about the ancient Greek text are in order here. First, the ancient manuscripts with which translators work are composed in *scriptio continua*, continuous script. There are no spaces between words, no punctuation marks, no distinctions between capital and lower-case letters. (Chapter and verse numbers were introduced in the sixteenth century). The other features are judgments made by modern translators of different English versions. So, if you were to read the ancient text and it were in English, the beginning of John might look like this:

INTHEBEGIN

NINGWASTH

EWORDANDT

HEWORDWAS

WITHGODAN

Second, the phrase that the NRSV translates "he was born blind" does not actually appear in the Greek text at all. The Greek text says this (I will leave out the capitals and punctuation to be truer to the text): "neither this one sinned nor his parents but in order that the works of God might be revealed in him we must work the works of the one who sent me while it is day night is coming when no one can work." Notice the difference in the following two translations of verses 3–4, first the NRSV and then my own.

> Jesus answered,
> "Neither this man nor his parents sinned;
> he was born blind so that God's works might be revealed in him.
> We must work the works of him who sent me while it is day;
> night is coming when no one can work." (NRSV)

> Jesus answered,
> "Neither this man nor his parents sinned.
> [He was born blind]. (The brackets indicate that this sentence is not in the Greek text. If you choose to include it, you should do so only as a matter of fact statement. He was born blind. Stuff happens. Or, even better, just leave it out as it's not in the Greek text at all.)
> In order that God's works might be revealed in him,
> we must work the works of him who sent me while it is day.
> Night is coming when no one can work." (my trans.)

These are two very different construals of the text. Reading the text the way I present it, we see Jesus moving away from an obsession with determining whose fault the man's impairment was, whether of the man, the parents, or God. It is simply a fact: the man was born blind. The reality is, he continues to be blind at that moment. While the disciples busy themselves with an academic exercise in theological hairsplitting, here sits a person (a person, not a "case") with an impairment. Even if they were able to determine whose fault it is, it does not change the fact that the man cannot see. Jesus turns their (stiff?) necks away from speculating about the past, focuses their gaze on the person in front of them, and asks them to consider whether or not they are going to work for and with God or—as we see later in the story in the case of the Pharisees—they are going to work for themselves and against God.

Put yourself in the place of the disciples. You show up, you see this interesting case, and you discuss it at length. Let's say you are, in fact, able to decide whose fault it is that the man is blind. How do your musings make his life better in any way? You may get to feel vindicated about being theologically correct, but you've done nothing to help the other person. You have only helped yourself. Jesus calls us to show up, assess the situation in an honest, other-oriented way, and ask, "Where is God in this situation, and how do I help this person move into God's future story for *them*?" It's not always about *us* and our theological satisfaction.

And here's another thing. We seem to have a tendency to look to the past when trying to deal with the present. The disciples look to the past to determine how the present situation came about. But Jesus turns their heads from the past and trains their eyes on the present. Their fixation on the past in no way informs the present situation and, in fact, keeps them from dealing with reality, while they go off on a flight of fancy to the past about whose fault this is.

We will see this pattern again in chapter 11 with Mary and Martha. Jesus has strong orders for his disciples (and that includes us!): we are to work the works of God. God is in the business of making a way out of no way, of creation, of abundant life. Indeed, this is the Gospel in which Jesus says to his disciples (us): "Very truly, I tell you, the one who believes in me will also do the works that I do and, in fact, will do greater works than these, because I am going to the

Father" (14:12). Greater works than Jesus himself? Wow. I guess it's time to get to work.

Jesus definitively declares and demonstrates that, for his part, he sides with God. We have already heard about light (1:8) and works (4:34; 5:34 describes the guy in chap. 9; 5:36 Jesus' works). Remember, in John the "I am" statements are usually tied to particular "signs" (called "miracles" in other Gospels, but never in John). So it's not surprising that in chapter 8 Jesus says, "I am the light of the world," and the next sign that he does is to give sight to the man born blind.

Once again (cf. 1:1), the author alludes to the creation accounts of Genesis. Why does Jesus take earth and mix it with his saliva to effect this healing? Presumably, he could heal this man without touching him and without using the stuff of earth. But Jesus identifies himself with the creative, life-giving force of God as recounted in Genesis and reminds us, once again, that the stuff of earth and the stuff of heaven are unequivocally enmeshed; the stuff of earth (water, bread, mud, fish, Scripture) has the power to reveal God to us. After all, God, with Jesus, has created it all anyway.

Jesus tells the man to go wash in the pool of Siloam (v. 7). Of course, whenever we see water, Christians think of baptism (see Nicodemus in chap. 3; 7:38; and chap. 19, where blood and water come out of Jesus' side). In 2004, the pool of Siloam mentioned here was uncovered; it can be visited (with some effort) today. It's not accidental that the man born blind who is presented as a hero of the faith is associated with a pool whose name means "sent," because repeatedly Jesus himself and his disciples are those who are sent.

Scene 2: What Do the Neighbors Think? (9:8–12)

The rest of the story narrates reactions of various people to the healing: the man, the neighbors, the parents, and the religious authorities. The neighbors are thrown off-kilter by the healing. The man healed confounds their tidy categories so much that they can't even decide if he's the same man they knew before. Rather than celebrate and praise God, they work to keep him in his place so that their world is not shaken. The man refuses their binary categories and claims an integrated identity with his response: "I am" (*egō eimi*; "the man" does not appear in the text but has been inserted by the translators). That is, he is *both* the very man who used to sit and beg *and* something more than that, all at once. For John, moving into one's future story with God does not mean denying one's former life (see chaps. 4 and 21). Healing involves owning our past, not denying it, fearing it, or clinging to the shame of it.

The "I am" (*egō eimi*) statements constitute one of the most famous and celebrated features of the Gospel's conveyance of its christological claims (as discussed in the previous chapter). Use of the "I am" here associates him with Jesus and is a bold expression of identity. The fact that he had to keep on saying "I am" (the verb used indicates repetition) implies an ongoing interaction and interrogation.

The neighbors repeatedly demand an explanation. Healing usually has social ramifications. When one person receives healing, others want to know whether it will disturb their own equilibrium, sense of identity, sense of what's possible or not possible, or sense of power. This is true in both the first century and the twenty-first. We will see the same fear and lack of support from the parents and the religious leaders.

Scene 3: Pharisees (9:13–17)

The reader now learns that, as in chapter 5, Jesus performs the cure/miracle on the Sabbath. On the surface, the conversation appears to be about the miraculous cure, as verse 14 repeats that he "opened his eyes," and verse 15 has the Pharisees continually ask him "how he had received his sight." The verb is in the imperfect tense, stressing the ongoing ordeal to which the man is being subjected. He stands firmly confident and unabashed as he summarizes his experience, shares his testimony, and becomes an evangelist. Like the neighbors, instead of celebrating with the man and giving glory to God, the Pharisees bicker among themselves, but this time about the identity of Jesus rather than that of the man born blind, so that the story transitions to the question of whether *Jesus* is a sinner, not whether the man is a sinner. The man is now called to testify. Whereas he first identifies Jesus merely as a person (*anthrōpos*), he now reveals a deeper understanding of who Jesus is: a prophet. To call Jesus a prophet is to ascribe to him religious authority; recall that Moses, Elijah, and Elisha all performed healings.

Scene 4: The Parent Trap (9:18–23)

The religious leaders next interrogate the man's parents in order to build a case against Jesus. To say that the parents fail to support their son in any way, as he attempts to negotiate the power structures of his society, is an understatement. They cower, fearing the cost of advocating for their son, while the formerly blind man speaks truth to power. No matter—he is probably used to standing alone and against. Apparently his parents fail him.

Scene 5: Pharisees, Round 2 (9:24–34)

This passage drips with irony based on the verb "to know" (*ginōskō*). These Pharisees claim to know that Jesus is a sinner, and they want to bully the man into siding with them and against Jesus. The man pleads ignorance concerning their academic debate but insists on what he *does* know: Jesus did, in fact, open his eyes (literally and metaphorically). They continue to badger him, but he knows that they are impervious to the gospel, so he has a bit of fun at their expense. He acts up.

As usual, acting up to the powers that be brings swift castigation, threat, and rejection. They attempt to dissociate Jesus from Moses in order to make the man choose Moses. They base this on their so-called knowledge. Remember that Jesus has already addressed this false dichotomy between Jesus and Moses, as well as Jesus and Scripture, in 5:39–47:

> "You search the scriptures because you think that in them you have eternal life; and it is they that testify on my behalf. Yet you refuse to come to me to have life. I do not accept glory from human beings. But I know that you do not have the love of God in you. I have come in my Father's name, and you do not accept me; if another comes in his own name, you will accept him. How can you believe when you accept glory from one another and do not seek

> the glory that comes from the one who alone is God? Do not think that I will accuse you before the Father; your accuser is Moses, on whom you have set your hope. If you believed Moses, you would believe me, for he wrote about me. But if you do not believe what he wrote, how will you believe what I say?"

I guess they needed to hear what David Bartlett, American Baptist minister and dear friend, is fond of saying: "We are a Jesus-believing people who have the Bible, not a Bible-believing people who have Jesus." Don't lose sight of the forest for the trees.

The irony remains thick about who knows what. The leaders declare that they do not know where Jesus is from and base their rejection of him upon that fact. The experienced reader of John knows that the question of where Jesus is from (above), by whom he has been sent (God), and where he is going (to God) is paramount and that the leaders condemn themselves by accidentally speaking the truth, because, in fact, they do not know where Jesus is from and they do not care to learn the truth about him. Both what they do know and what they do not know indict them. The man commandeers the floor and presents a logical, theological argument. He gets downright saucy, taunting them. To paraphrase: "Wow—your so-called knowledge is keeping you from seeing the glory of God at work. Your knowledge is too small to make room for the wondrous works of God. What a shame." They try to subordinate the man with the statement: "We . . . but you . . ." He dismisses their move and in verses 31 and 33 declares, "We know that God does not listen to sinners, but he does listen to one who worships him and obeys his will [which the leaders are patently failing to do] . . . . If this man were not from God, he could do nothing" [let alone miraculously provide sight].

They immediately dissociate themselves once again, using categories of "you" and "us." The plot of the entire narrative of John's Gospel (beginning with 1:11: "He came to what was his own, and his own people did not accept him") involves the quest of the religious leaders to disable Jesus because of his refusal to accept the unjust, death-dealing, keep-people-in-their-place society. When this man who was formerly blind chooses to side with Jesus, they move to ad hominem attack that focuses on the man's sin, just as the disciples had done at the beginning. The verb used in verse 34 for driving the man out (*ekballō*) is quite violent; it is the same word used for driving out demons. The gatekeepers are not amused.

Scene 6: Fade to Black (9:35–41)

In the final scene, Jesus once again initiates the action between the man and himself, and the man's insight about Jesus' revelation as the Son of Man is disclosed: "You have seen (*horaō*) him." So complete is the man's understanding and commitment that he now calls Jesus not "person" or even "prophet" but "Lord" (*kyrios*) and declares his belief. Given that John clearly states that the purpose of the Gospel is to engender belief (20:31), the man perfectly exemplifies the call to discipleship. His willingness to engage Jesus and ask questions about his identity (reminiscent of the Samaritan woman earlier) leads him finally to worship (*proskyneō*) Jesus (v. 38).

Jesus then speaks for the benefit of the Pharisees when he says: "I came into this world for judgment so that those who do not see may see, and those who do see may become blind" (v. 39). The reader is reminded of Jesus' earlier statements about seeing, light, and darkness: "'Very truly, I tell you, no one can see the kingdom of God without being born from above'" (3:3). Clearly, and ironically, the man born blind sees the kingdom of God. Further, Jesus says, "And this is the judgment, that the light has come into the world, and people loved darkness rather than light because their deeds were evil. For all who do evil hate the light and do not come to the light, so that their deeds may not be exposed. But those who do what is true come to the light, so that it may be clearly seen that their deeds have been done in God" (3:19–21).

Jesus, the light, has come into the world and is shining in the faces of the religious leaders. They hate the light and want to do the evil deed of disabling Jesus through death. The man born blind sees the light and does the work of God by believing in Jesus. The Pharisees intuit that Jesus refers to them, and they find it incredible that they, given all of their knowledge, status, and power, should be considered blind (which [unfortunately] is a code word for "ignorant" here: as the saying goes—"there are none so blind as those who will not see"). Jesus disrupts the analogy by indicating that those born blind (as was the man they have just accused of being a sinner) are not sinners. Rather, those who stand judged are the physically sighted who claim too much for themselves with respect to insight, and commit the sin of willful ignorance—not to mention abuse of power (see 15:22) and the demeaning of those without physical sight.

Some Conclusions

Mountains of material have been written on John 9, because it's so rich with interpretive possibilities and life application. Let me summarize some of the points we've covered in this chapter:

1. All translation is interpretation. Remember that your English Bible has come to you through a long process and you are free to question the decisions of the translators and editors.
2. Christian life is ironic.
3. We are always both our former and our present selves, and that's a fact to be celebrated, not avoided or hidden away in shame.
4. Having repeated encounters with Jesus leads to deep revelation. At first the man born blind (who is nameless like the Samaritan woman) calls Jesus a man, then a prophet; finally he worships him as the Son of Man and Lord.
5. Jesus takes initiative to heal us. Jesus is always the one coming-into-the-world such that the phrase essentially constitutes a title for Jesus in John. Jesus seeks us even when we are not seeking Jesus.
6. We are called to testify about the works of Jesus, no matter who we are, even when it means speaking truth to power. This man was a blind, uneducated beggar with no name or status. Yet his story continues to call us to discipleship thousands of years later.

If I had to list three general take-aways from the story, here's what I would highlight.

First, trust your experience and don't let anyone tame it or take it away from you. Maybe the details of your experience with God are unorthodox and color outside the lines. Maybe you are an unlikely candidate for testifying to the gospel. If so, you will relate to your brother in chapter 9. By the way, you can also see Galatians 3:1–5, where Paul helps the Galatians embrace and celebrate their experience of Christ in the face of some Bible thumpers who are trying to undermine their truth. Of course, our experiences are to be shared and deciphered in community; but be bold with owning your story of God's action in your own life.

Second, let's not say stupid stuff about sin and suffering. Don't say things that assume a connection between sin and suffering. Instead, let's do the work Jesus has called us to do. Let's show up to places of need; listen to the story of the one who is suffering; stop pretending that we know the answer to everything; and reorient those who are dehumanizing the person in front of us (as the disciples were doing with the man born blind when they turned him into an academic exercise instead of a person). Let's engage the actual person (rather than talking about the person or "their kind") and ask good questions that allow us to understand their situation and see how God is calling us to accompany them into their future story. That's the work to which we've been called. If Jesus can say, "Indeed, God did not send the Son into the world to condemn the world, but in order that the world might be healed through him" (3:17), then surely our task as Jesus' followers who have been empowered to do "greater works than [Jesus] himself did" (14:12) involves healing, not condemning.

Finally, remember (and remind others) that God is *always* making a way out of no way. So always, always, be an agent of *hope*. If a message is not marked by hope, it may be many things, but it is, by definition, not Christian.

Questions for Reflection

Is your community a John 9 community?

If I had to list four characteristics of a community that takes John 9 seriously, here's what I'd say: (1) It's a community of individuals who seek to encounter Christ for the purpose of transformation. Transformation is an ongoing process. The more you encounter Christ, the more you understand who he is: man, prophet, Son of Man, and Lord worthy of worship. (2) It's a community that judges rightly. Who's really a sinner? Why is a person struggling? Is it his fault or the system's in this case? (3) It's a community that is open to critique. Do our established understandings shut out the chance to see God at work? Are we humble enough to admit that for now we see in a mirror dimly, as Paul says? (4) It's a bold, fearless community. The parents do not stand in solidarity with the outsider, and they don't confess Christ because fear has gripped them. What do we do?

Chapter 6

Waiting for Wading at Bethesda, Stirring Up or Standing Down?

John 5

*I*n chapter 9 we saw John correct our facile, erroneous assumption that suffering is related to sin. Sometimes suffering happens, and it's not our fault or even anyone else's.

But John is never simplistic. In chapter 5, we are confronted with the fact that sometimes we do cause or contribute to our own suffering or stand in the way of our own healing. I want to be very careful here to stress that we should never engage in "blaming the victim." Each person's suffering must be addressed on an individual basis, and that person must be the one to consider and name the nature of her or his suffering. However, the story helps us to ask ourselves and those who seek our counsel some good questions to use in the discernment process of articulating the nature of our pain and the way(s) forward.

You may wonder why I'm treating chapter 5 after chapter 9 rather than before it. First, I'm putting chapter 9 first because there is a greater tendency for people to automatically connect suffering with sin, and I want to correct that tendency emphatically. Second, in chapter 9 we see one of John's heroes who models good discipleship. He gets healed, encounters Jesus repeatedly, worships Jesus, speaks truth to power, takes risks for the gospel, and truly embraces the abundant life God gives. Now that we have the good example, it will be easier to see why the man in chapter 5 may not be the best example of Christian discipleship from John's perspective.

In what follows, I will first offer one common approach to the text and then view it from a different perspective—that of Disability Studies.

Interpretation #1: One Typical Approach

This cure story immediately follows the one where the father exemplifies a faithful response to Jesus' curing of his son's illness (4:46–54). We found the man in chapter 9 at the pool of Siloam. In chapter 5 we find the man who was ill for thirty-eight years at another pool in Jerusalem, this time the pool of Bethesda. Since it served as a hospital of sorts, it is not surprising that "a crowd of people who were weak/sickly" lay there (my trans.). The NRSV calls these people "invalids." Of course, the heteronyms *in*valid and in*valid* should not be lost on the modern reader concerned about disability issues. More about that later.

At verse 6, Jesus asks the unnamed man if he wills or wishes (the Greek word *thelō* means both "will" and "wish") to be healthy. On the face of it, it is a stupid or insensitive question: Who does *not* wish to be healthy? Notice, however, that the man does not actually ever answer the question; he says neither yes nor no. Many readers of this Gospel understand this to be the question of all questions because unless one has the will to be well, the likelihood of wellness remains slim. What one wills or wishes matters. In fact, it would appear that some people find their equilibrium precisely in misery. Sometimes our sense of identity is based upon our sense of weakness, pain, or illness. If we do not actually wish or will to become healthy, it might be difficult for anyone, including Jesus, to help us to do so.

Of all the amazing things Jesus does, he excels at asking good questions, questions that drive us to the very core of ourselves and the situations that we find ourselves in or create for ourselves. I hope we all have at least one friend who can ask us the hardest questions about our choices, our habits, all of it, within the context of grace and "a love that will not let us go." And I hope it's mutual.

Does the man in chapter 5 wish to be made well? The evidence is not in his favor. First, he produces a litany of excuses: I have no one to put me into the pool just at the right time; when I do try to get into the pool, someone else gets there first. If the man in chapter 9 represents baptism (by actually entering the water), John may be contrasting this man with the other by showing that he does not go into the water (i.e., he does not get baptized, he does *not* become a follower). Notice also that the Samaritan woman accepts the offer of living water. This man never makes it into the stirred-up waters.

Second, he does not seem interested in establishing relationships or finding a community.

Third, he never declares that he wants to be made well (though he readily follows Jesus' orders).

Finally, though Jesus grants him healing, he shows no sign of gratitude, transformation, or understanding (unlike the royal official at 4:53). We may imagine that he will end up right back by the pool, drowning in his self-chosen illness, totally unlike the man born blind in chapter 9. He takes no risks for the gospel but protects his own interests at the expense of Jesus. Unlike the Samaritan woman and the man born blind, he does not proclaim Jesus to be a prophet, Messiah, or Lord, and he does not invite others to experience Jesus for themselves.

Jesus commands the man to stand up and walk. The fact that the whole event occurs on a Sabbath (a recurring theme in John: 5:9–10, 16, 18; 7:22–23; 9:14, 16; 19:31; 20:1, 19) antagonizes the religious authorities (gatekeepers of said Sabbath), who accost the man who had received therapy/been healed (*therapeuō*). Just as the man took no responsibility for his illness, he takes no responsibility for his healing. He immediately blames the incident on the person (*anthrōpos*) who directed him, a person whom he does not know (and does not seem interested in getting to know any better). These are apparently damning facts. First, in John, those who do not grasp Jesus' full identity refer to him merely as an *anthrōpos*, culminating in Pilate's famous dictum: "Behold, the *anthrōpos*" (19:5). Second, the verb "to know" (*ginōskō*) serves to mark insiders and outsiders in the Fourth Gospel. Insiders know; outsiders do not. The fact that the man confesses that he does not know Jesus implies that he does not become a disciple of Jesus and, in fact, serves as an example of failed discipleship.

Once again, Jesus takes it upon himself to approach the man in verse 14. He finds the man in the temple, of all places, and declares: "Behold you have become healthy. No longer keep sinning, in order that nothing worse happens to you" (author's translation). The command occurs in the second person singular (you, singular) present imperative. The present implies ongoing, habitual action. As controversial and problematic as Jesus' command might be here for modern readers, Jesus assumes this man to be an ongoing sinner of some sort. Note that the man's reaction to his cure is not one of gratitude or discipleship. Rather, he tattles to the antagonistic religious authorities with whom Jesus has already clashed in the temple (2:13–16). As a direct, causal result of the man's actions (*dia touto,* 5:16), the religious authorities persecute Jesus for curing on the Sabbath. At this point, the narrative morphs into a Sabbath controversy story focused upon Jesus' identity and authority vis-à-vis God.

When you picture this man five years later, where do you see him? I wonder if he ended up right back by the pool. Let's face it. Sometimes there are apparent benefits to remaining ill. For one thing, no one expects anything from us. We don't have any real responsibilities. I was discussing this story with a seven-year-old one time and the seven-year-old said, "It's like if you say you're sick. You don't have to go to school and do all that work." That's *exactly* what it can be like, I think.

So I invite us to think through this text and live through it. Do you wish to be made well? It involves change. It involves adopting a new persona to a degree. If you're in a family or a web of relationships, it means potential rupture of those relationships as you step out into health and mature past your assigned role in the family drama. It can cost something, and something dear and seemingly essential (like the Samaritan woman's water jar). All may feel lost when, actually, all is gained. Truly. So come, let us be made well through Jesus Christ, who lived and died and lives again for our sake.

Interpretation #2: The Importance of a Disability Lens

I concluded the interpretation above by noting that the man at Bethesda provides a negative example for readers in at least two ways. First, he represents failed discipleship. He encounters Jesus by a potential baptismal pool, but he never enters the baptismal waters, so to speak. By the end of the narrative, not only does he not follow Jesus; he works against Jesus by implicating him to the religious authorities. Second, he appears to represent those who suffer impairment as a result of their own sinful behavior.

Almost every passage in John could be (and has been) interpreted in numerous ways. In this book I try not to go in too many directions with each passage, as that would be overwhelming, perhaps confusing; for sure it would make for a book that is too long and expensive for the publisher's approval. But in this case I want to offer another angle on this passage, because there's an important conversation going on at present about the Bible and disability, a conversation that has not yet reached the church widely. In a new book, *Disability and the Bible: A Commentary*,[1] I have a lengthy essay on the Gospel of John and 1, 2, and 3 John that asks, "From a disability perspective, what are the promises and pitfalls of these texts with respect to ancient audiences and later interpreters? That is, in what ways does the text have liberative potential and in what ways does it present obstacles for those seeking abundant life (Jn. 10:10)?"[2]

So I want to use chapter 5 as a representative case to showcase some of the issues to think about. Is there any way that chapter 5 might be useful or suggestive for those who seek justice for people with disabilities? Or is it unhelpful in this regard? Or both?

Definitions

As with every area of specialization, there is specialized vocabulary. Hence a few definitions are in order before we begin.

In Disability Studies it is customary to distinguish between impairment (a physiological, medical phenomenon) and disability (a social or cultural phenomenon). A society disables people with impairments when it refuses to take steps to ensure that all members of society have equal access to the benefits of that society, including education, transportation, employment, architecture that can be navigated, political power—all entitlements that people with "normate" bodies usually take for granted. A "normal" body is really just an idealized social construct. What does a "normal" body look like? Is it male? female? transgendered? Is it black? white? brown? Is it short? tall? Does it have freckles or not? You see, it (a normal body) doesn't

1. *Disability and the Bible: A Commentary*, ed. Sarah J. Melcher, Mikeal C. Parsons, and Amos Yong (Waco, TX: Baylor University Press, forthcoming).

2. Clark-Soles, "Disability in the Johannine Literature (Gospel of John, 1–3 John, Apocalypse)," in *Disability and the Bible*.

exist in real life; it's a made-up idea. The technical term "normate" body is often used instead of "normal" to indicate this fact.

Sometimes the word "disability" is used synonymously with the word "impairment." But, more technically speaking, an impairment is a deviation from the normate body that may or may not constitute a problem for the impaired person. The impairment may or may not cause pain; the person may not find a cure necessary if there is no pain or suffering. The word "disability" is often reserved for the suffering and injustice that come from the way society treats a person with an impairment. In other words, society disables people with impairments. So someone may be born with no legs and need a wheelchair to move from place to place. He or she may be in no physical pain. The disability arises from the fact that curbs make it impossible for those in wheelchairs to access the same facilities that "nondisabled" people (sometimes referred to as TABs, temporarily able-bodied) take for granted, including civic buildings, buses, trains, even churches (especially chancels and choir lofts). Or a person born blind (as in chap. 9) may be marginalized as a sinner because of the way a society or religion construes reality and God's favor or disfavor.

Another crucial matter of definition relates to the language of "cure" and "healing." Cure refers to the elimination of impairment and is experienced at the individual level. Healing refers to the change in a person who has experienced integration and reconciliation to self, God, and the community. Healing may or may not involve a cure. Just as impairment is experienced on an individual basis, so is a cure. Just as a disability is a communally imposed limitation, so also healing entails a communally based liberation.

Questions Raised

From a disability perspective, John 5 raises some questions. First, both the person and the disability are *erased* in a number of ways. He has no name, and no specific details are given about his impairment or how he became impaired. In a sense, he figures not as a person but as pawn in an able-bodied narrative about Jesus revealing his own identity, power, authority, and ability as God's agent. He is useful to the normate interpreter only insofar as he has a disability. The encounter functions primarily as an episode in Jesus' escalating controversy with the religious authorities. In fact, the text launches into a christological monologue in 5:19–47. The man himself is a cipher. As Kathy Black notes in her wonderful book *A Healing Homiletic: Preaching and Disability*:

> We tend to use them [the people in the biblical stories who are disabled] as objects to make some other point. The problem with this is that persons with disabilities today likewise find themselves treated as objects. Health care, education, employment, social services—all the basic institutions of our society often view persons with disabilities as objects to be dealt with, rather than as subjects that have something to contribute.[3]

This is an example of what David Mitchell and Sharon Snyder have termed "narrative prosthesis." They explain:

> Our notion of narrative prosthesis evolves out of this specific recognition: a narrative issues to resolve or correct—to "prostheticize" in David Wills's sense of the term—a deviance marked as improper to a social context. A simple schematic of narrative structure might run thus: first, a deviance or marked difference is exposed to a reader; second, a narrative consolidates the need for its own existence by calling for an explanation of the deviation's origins and formative consequences; third, the deviance is brought from the periphery of concerns to the center of the story to come; and fourth, the remainder of the story rehabilitates or fixes the deviance in some manner. This fourth step of the repair of deviance may involve an obliteration of the difference through a "cure," the rescue of the despised object from social censure, the extermination of the deviant as a purification of the social body, or the revaluation of an alternative mode of being. Since what we now call disability has been historically narrated as that which characterizes a body as deviant from shared norms of bodily appearance and ability, disability has functioned throughout history as one of the most marked and remarked upon differences that originates

3. Kathy Black, *A Healing Homiletic: Preaching and Disability* (Nashville: Abingdon Press, 1996), 13.

> the act of storytelling. Narratives turn signs of cultural deviance into textually marked bodies.[4]

This leads to a second issue: For whose sake was the man cured in this story? Jesus asks if the man wills the cure; the man never says that he wills the cure, but Jesus cures him anyway. Is this an opportunistic move on Jesus' part? A normate interpretation assumes that cure is the goal of all who have impairments of various sorts, so that the disabled person's body will resemble more closely the normate body that the society deems as ideal. But some people with impairments are not, in fact, obsessed with achieving a normate body. Rather, they maintain that creation radiates diversity, that bodies come in all different shapes, sizes, colors, forms, configurations, and that there is no reason to value one more than the other.

What if, instead of focusing upon curing differently abled bodies to bring them in line with a cultural ideal, a society began to honor the true diversity of embodied existence and valued that diversity, resulting in creating societies whose architecture (literal and metaphorical) accommodated—no, celebrated—that wide variety as testifying to the full image of God, rather than valuing only one type of body (so-called "able")? In a society driven by the medical model, which sees impairment as a problem to be eradicated, judgment looms large upon those who do not cooperate in the effort to "overcome" their difference. This is one of the places where vigorous debate ensues in the disability community about issues of "passing" and the place of "otherness."

Third, both ancient and modern interpreters reflect what Warren Carter cites as a "physiognomic consciousness" that "posits a correlation between physical appearance and moral character and shifts attention to matters of character. Thus it focuses on physical ugliness and somatic deformity in that they represent evil, vice, stupidity and low status."[5] Jesus makes this move, according to Carter, when he insists that the man's illness is connected to poor moral character. Some illnesses are. Carter's review of commentaries on this passage

4. David T. Mitchell and Sharon L. Snyder, *Narrative Prosthesis: Disability and the Dependencies of Discourse* (Ann Arbor: University of Michigan Press, 2000), 53–54.

5. Warren Carter, "'The blind, lame, and paralyzed' (John 5:3): John's Gospel, Disability Studies, and Postcolonial Perspectives," in Candida R. Moss and Jeremy Schipper, *Disability Studies and Biblical Literature* (New York: Palgrave Macmillan, 2011), 130.

demonstrates that this is a common approach. Such interpretive moves are made by the likes of B. F. Westcott, who opines that

> the paralyzed man *acquiesces* in his condition by failing to get into the "stirred up" waters in time to be healed. Marked by apathy, he lacks willingness to "make any vigorous effort to gain relief." Raymond Brown describes him as marked by "obtuseness," an "unimaginative approach to the curative waters," "a chronic inability to seize opportunity," "real dullness," and "persistent naiveté." C. H. Dodd thinks that the man "refused to make use of [Torah's] means of grace;" he "has not the will" to live, and offers a "feeble excuse" for not getting into the water.[6]

One of the chief problems with this physiognomic approach is, again, erasure of actual physical disability. That is to say, the focus becomes centered on the man's (supposed) character or (speculative) psychological motivations. Unfortunately, when that happens, the fact of the man's *actual* physical disability and the social, spiritual, political, economic realities or consequences of that fact are rendered invisible. This is a problematic interpretive approach that erases the importance of those realities for contemporary individuals, communities, and societies. But the problem is generated by the Johannine text itself.

Fourth, as I argued in the treatment of chapter 9, linking sin with impairment can be a dangerous, destructive habit. A connection may be possible in particular cases, but such is not inevitable. Similarly, tying salvation and forgiveness of sins to a "cure" is also problematic. It can imply that disabled persons who remain "uncured" remain unsaved or unforgiven or lacking in faith or, in fact, unhealed. This can victimize the victim, falsely identify disabled persons as victims, and make temporarily able-bodied people feel superior in body and soul. Remember, healing and cure are not synonymous.

Wynn: Chapter 5 as a Negative Example of Individual Sin

Kerry Wynn admits that there is no denying Jesus' bald connection between sin and disability in the case of the man in chapter 5. Wynn

6. Carter, "'The blind, lame, and paralyzed,'" 131.

begins his essay with this statement: "The two most common assumptions in popular theology that marginalize people with disabilities are (1) disability is caused by sin, and (2) if one has enough faith, one will be healed."[7] In his comparative analysis between the man in chapter 5 and the man born blind in chapter 9, he argues that the relationship between sin and disability in each narrative has to do with the person's *reaction* to his disability. In the case of the man in chapter 5, Wynn writes:

> The man who had been disabled for thirty-eight years is located in the institutional healthcare system of the normate society. It is no accident that "Bethesda" is a popular name for hospitals. This is not to say that curative pools and modern medicine do not have a vital role to play in the reality of disability in the first and the twenty-first centuries. The problem is that after thirty-eight years he is still looking for a miracle cure and life has passed him by. He has bought into the role of the helpless dependent and the normate society has affirmed him in this role. That a normate society still affirms that role today can be seen in modern interpretations of this passage.[8]

The man has acquiesced to the shallow, myopic values of the dominant culture (represented by the religious authorities), rather than adopting Jesus' alternative way, truth, and life that incarnationally affirms the value and legitimacy of a wide variety of embodied existences.

As with numerous other stories in John, like John 9, interpreters associate this story with baptismal themes. The man never makes the healing waters before Jesus arrives and never enters the baptismal waters after. "He has failed to heed Jesus' admonition not to sin any more by remaining subject to normate society and thus 'something worse' has happened to him."[9]

Carter: Chapter 5 as Negative Example of Systemic, Structural Sin

Warren Carter views the man more sympathetically than Wynn as he addresses this passage through a postcolonial lens, arguing that

7. Kerry H. Wynn, "Johannine Healings and the Otherness of Disability," *Perspectives in Religious Studies* 34 (2007): 61-75, (61).
8. Wynn, "Johannine Healings," 65.
9. Wynn, "Johannine Healings," 70.

the man is disabled by the Roman Empire and his own society, a territory occupied intensively by Rome. As feminists and womanists know deeply, the politics of a society get mapped onto real bodies, particularly bodies considered deviant from the normate body of a given society. "These bodies [disabled bodies in John's Gospel] reveal the lie of imperial claims to be a force for wholeness and healing even while they compete with and imitate this imperial vision. John constructs an alternative world that participates in, imitates, and contests Roman power."[10]

Carter creatively analogizes from Frantz Fanon's *The Wretched of the Earth*, whose work is set in the context of French rule in Algeria, and Salmon Rushdie's novel *Midnight's Children*, whose context is British imperial rule over India and its consequences. Imperial powers, both ancient and modern, posture as providers of health and peace, whose leaders are often referred to as saviors. In truth, imperial powers disable people in multifarious ways from very basic needs such as access to nutritious food, clean water, medicine, sanitary living conditions, education, employment, and social mobility. Empires send their own people to war, where they sustain disabilities and invade other groups, where they inflict disabilities. Carter interrogates the narrative in chapter 5 to discern how the man's disabilities relate to empire:

> In Fanon and Rushdie's psychosomatic framing, blindness and paralysis ambiguously exhibit the overwhelming power of imperializing agents along with the reticence of the subjugated. Does the inability of the paralyzed man to move in John 5 attest overwhelming paralyzing imperial power and/or does it attest the subjugated's refusal to be moved? Does the inability of the blind man in John 9 to see attest overwhelming "shock-and-awe," blinding, imperial power (military power and every imperial structure) and/or does it attest a means whereby the subjugated refuses to acknowledge power?[11]

While most commentators worry about the link between individual sin and disability, Carter asks the important, larger question of the role of social systems in disabling people: "Who sinned?

10. Carter, "'The blind, lame, and paralyzed,'" 129–30.
11. Carter, "'The blind, lame, and paralyzed,'" 136.

At least in part, the empire and every and any politico-economic-cultural societal system that deprives people of adequate food resources and creates unjust living conditions that damage and disable people. Imperializing power and practices—whether ancient or modern, governments or multinationals—should come with a warning: they can be bad for people's health."[12]

Conclusion

The man in chapter 5 raises questions for those in (post)modern societies. Is this man truly a whining victim, or are commentators blaming the victim? If he is repulsive to behold, is it because of his own weak character, or is it a result of what the system has done to him? Of course, all colonizing agents know that the best way to keep a people subjugated is to have them internalize messages of nonagency and weakness and worthlessness and simultaneously to have the subjugated people mimic the values of the colonizers, such that to "make it" means to associate with and be what those in power most respect: strong, able-bodied people.

Where Caesar fails, Jesus can deliver. He can heal and save (and, perhaps incidentally, he also cures). He can provide true peace based on justice, and he can bring abundant, eternal life. In Jesus, not Caesar, one may find healing. The man in chapter 5 may be cured, but he does not appear to be healed. What does this mean for our own lives today, individually and communally? How is the risen Christ addressing us, addressing you, through this story?

12. Carter, "'The blind, lame, and paralyzed,'" 145.

Chapter 7

From Accusation to Acclamation

John 11

John 11 opens with these words: "Now a certain man was ill, Lazarus of Bethany, the village of Mary[1] and her sister Martha. . . . So the sisters sent a message to Jesus, 'Lord, he whom you love is ill.'" Chapter 11 is often called "The Raising of Lazarus." It's true that Lazarus is raised along the way, but Lazarus never actually speaks in the passage. Martha, in fact, is the one who engages Jesus at a deep theological level and receives one of the great "I am" statements from Jesus (this should sound like a familiar pattern if you've read the story of the Samaritan woman in John 4). "The Confession of Martha" might be a better title.

Let's take a closer look. Word is sent to Jesus from the sisters that Lazarus is ill. Jesus does not rush to the scene. Instead, he seems to tarry, saying, "This illness does not lead to death; rather it is for God's glory, so that the Son of God may be glorified through it." We the readers are supposed to understand that what is about to take place will show us God's glory and that Jesus is the Son of God. Verse 5 is particularly interesting because it emphasizes Jesus' love. It understands our confusion, because it says that although he loved them, he did not behave in what they (and we) might understand as a loving way (rushing to their sides immediately) but instead intentionally waited. How do you react to this? Notice also that Martha is

1. It's important to note that this Mary is *not* Mary Magdalene, is *not* a sinner, and is *not* a prostitute. There seems to be a lot of confusion about this. I sort out all of the Marys and all of the women who anoint Jesus in *Engaging the Word* (Louisville, KY: Westminster John Knox Press, 2010), 36–42.

named first, her sister Mary is unnamed, and Lazarus is named last. This story is largely about Martha and, finally, you and me.

Jesus tells the disciples he's heading to Judea because that's where Martha, Mary, and Lazarus are. When studying the Gospel of John, you should regularly repeat this phrase: Geography is theology. Notice that in John whenever Jesus is in Galilee, life is splendid for him; but whenever he heads south to Judea, the ominous music begins to play in the background. The disciples try to talk sense into him, saying, "Rabbi, the Judeans [my trans.] were just now trying to stone you, and are you going there again?" (v. 8). Jesus insists upon going and speaks of awakening Lazarus. In typical Johannine fashion, the disciples are stuck on a literal level while Jesus is operating at a spiritual level. Listen to this:

> After saying this, he told them, "Our friend Lazarus has fallen asleep, but I'm going there to awaken him."
>
> The disciples said to him, "Lord, if he has fallen asleep, he'll be all right."
>
> Jesus, however, had been speaking about his death, but they thought that he was referring merely to sleep.
>
> Then Jesus told them plainly, "Lazarus is dead." (vv. 11–14)

He once again makes a statement that may sound both harsh and strange: harsh, because Jesus intentionally tarries, and strange, because he appears to allow the suffering of his beloved Martha, Mary, and Lazarus patently so that his disciples would believe. Again, how does that sit with you?

Thomas knows full well that Judea, the center of religious authority, is a dangerous place for Jesus. I love Thomas—I call him the Eeyore of the New Testament. Thomas is never optimistic but always resigned to loyal behavior. When he calls the group to go, it's not in an energetic Peter voice but an Eeyore voice: "Let us go too so that we may die with him" (v. 16; my trans.). I just love that guy!

As Jesus and the disciples arrive in Bethany, Martha rushes out to meet them—crazed with grief, I'm sure—while Mary stays at home. Listen closely to what Martha says to him (I'm willing to bet that you've said something similar; I know I have): "Lord, *if only* you had been here, my brother would not have died." If only, if only. How many hours a week, a month, a year, do we spend on the "if only" game? Our necks are craned to the past, fantasizing about what could have been, dreaming of would-be destinies. As if we could change the past. We can't. And neither can Martha. Her brother is dead. He's really dead. Rotting in a grave, stinking to high heaven. If only.

But look at how quickly she goes from what could have been in verse 21 to what will be in the sweet by-and-by: "'But even now I know that God will give you whatever you ask of him.' Jesus said to her, 'Your brother will rise again.' Martha said to him, 'I know that he will rise again in the resurrection on the last day'" (vv. 22–24).

At this point Martha is in danger of whiplash as she jerks her neck from gazing at the unresolved past to squinting toward the utopian future. But Jesus wants her to turn her face toward him and train her eyes on the very full, abundant present that is available here and now in his presence; so he declares, "*I am* the resurrection and the life. Those who believe in me, even though they die, will live, and everyone who lives and believes in me will never die. Do you believe this?" (vv. 25–26).

Now, to her credit, Martha is stating a sound doctrine from her own tradition about the coming Messiah in the future. But the doctrine is rather heady and vague for her and does not address her very real, immediate grief and concern. Sometimes doctrines can be that way. But Jesus aims to convince her by his living presence and person that resurrection and life are already available *now* to everyone who believes. He aims to convince you and me as well. Life is a key concept in the Gospel of John: abundant life, embodied life, eternal life, precious life. Some form of the word "life" or "living" occurs over fifty times in this Gospel, from beginning to end. Recall John 1:4: "In him was *life*, and the *life* was the light of all people." And John 20:31: "But these are written so that you may come to believe that Jesus is the Messiah, the Son of God, and that through believing you may have *life* in his name." And, of course, one of the most important verses in the Gospel, 10:10: "I came that they may have *life*, and have it abundantly." The life Jesus brings is available to all of us here and now. If we aren't living it, we may need to ask ourselves why.

Notice that Jesus never promises that believers won't die a physical death along the way. Jesus relativizes death; it is no longer ultimate. Eternal life—a certain *quality* of life marked by abundance, joy, peace, and love—is available now and will continue forever. Death does not and cannot interfere with any of that, because Jesus has cast out that power through his exaltation on the cross, whereby he accomplished his promise declared at 12:32: "And I, when I am lifted up from the earth, will draw all people to myself." *All* people, not just some. That includes you and me. On the other hand, there are people walking around us all the time who might as well be dead; they have not seized the abundant life readily available to them. This is what John is saying: there is living, and then there is *living*.

In the end, Martha absolutely "gets it"—so much so that she says: "Yes, Lord, I believe that you are the Messiah, the Son of God, the one coming into the world" (v. 27). Martha becomes a model disciple. She calls Jesus by the titles that matter to the author of John: Lord, Messiah, and Son of God (recall the thesis statement at 20:31). Remember that from the beginning of this story Jesus aimed to prove that he is the Son of God. Recall John 11:4: "This illness does not lead to death; rather it is for God's glory, so that the *Son of God* may be glorified through it." Martha understands who Jesus is and how that affects her life here and now and brings abundant, eternal life here and now. She even closes the confession by calling him "the one coming into the world." This title, unique to this Gospel, is very important. Already the opening chapter of John tells us this about Jesus: "The true light, which enlightens everyone, was coming into the world" (1:9). That's just part and parcel of who Jesus is: he is *always* the one coming into the world, every minute of every day, seeking us out. Every moment of every day is ripe with the promise of resurrection and life. The point is not to escape the world but to transform it such that it promotes the flourishing of all creation, the creation that God carefully orchestrated. God is always at work in the world, in embodied lives.

The rest of the story shows Lazarus, indeed, being raised in order to exemplify Jesus' authority over life and death. Jesus makes this point explicitly one chapter earlier where he declares: "I am the good shepherd" (10:11). In the midst of *that* discourse, Jesus declares: "For this reason the Father loves me, because I lay down my life *in order to take it up again*. No one takes it from me, but I lay it down of my own accord. I have power to lay it down, and I have power to take it up again" (10:17–18).

There's Something about Mary

Though chapter 11 is mostly Martha's story, Mary is not absent. She is named first in verse 1, and verse 2 points ahead to the next chapter, where she will get her fifteen minutes in the spotlight. This pointing ahead to a story that has not yet happened is a typical literary technique used by this author. It is called prolepsis (e.g., 3:24 and 6:71). The author also refers the reader back to events that have already occurred in the narrative; that is called analepsis (see 18:14 and 19:39). Remember that we are meant to read the whole Gospel, in order, like a novel, not just in pieces here and there pulled out of the narrative. It's a whole narrative universe, and each part really makes sense only in the context of the whole.

Both Martha and Mary send word to Jesus. In verse 5, Mary is unnamed. We next see her at verse 19, when we learn that some from their community had come to console them in their deep grief. Then Martha goes off to have her personal encounter with Jesus while Mary stays home.

After that, Martha tags Mary and says, "You're it. Jesus is calling for you, specifically." He still does that today, of course. I have to ask myself: Am I listening? Are you?

Now Mary has reached Jesus, and I imagine her body language to be at odds with her words. Sure, to show respect and homage, she falls at Jesus' feet. ("Knelt" [v. 32 NRSV] is not really correct, because it gives the impression of kneeling in worship as the magi did—*proskyneō*. In this instance, it's literally "fell or collapsed at his feet" (*piptō*) and implies a force and desperation that is not as dignified and controlled as "knelt.") But Mary has an issue with Jesus, the same one Martha had: "Lord, *if only* you had been here, such and such would have gone differently, would have gone the way it *should* have." That's the last we hear from Mary until she anoints Jesus.

Jesus, Lazarus, and Us

In verse 33 Jesus sees Mary weeping (*klaiō*) and her companions also weeping; this creates in him a strong reaction. The author uses two different verbs (*embrimaomai* and *tarassō*). The NRSV translates thus: "greatly disturbed in spirit and deeply moved." The CEB translates it as: "deeply disturbed and troubled." The same verb translated "disturbed" occurs again in verse 38. Scholars have extremely lively debate over what exactly Jesus is feeling here. Many think that the first phrase, translated by the NRSV "disturbed in spirit," reflects anger on Jesus' part. For example, Francis Moloney writes: "When Jesus sees Mary weeping, and 'the Jews' who are with her also weeping . . . , he is strangely moved. It is not compassion—or lack of it—that creates Jesus' being moved to anger in spirit and troubled. . . . As Jesus' public ministry draws to a close he is frustrated and angrily disappointed (*enebrimēsato*), and this is manifested in a deep, shuddering internal emotion (*etaraxen*)."[2] Is Jesus sad, depressed, disturbed, angry, troubled, or all of the above?

Verse 35 is famous for Jesus' show of emotion (not to mention that it's the shortest verse in the KJV Bible, so a favorite one for anyone tasked with memorizing a Bible verse!). He weeps. When Mary and "the Jews" do so, the common verb *klaiō* is used. When Jesus does it, the verb is *dakryō*. *Dakryō* appears nowhere else in the New Testament. It does appear in the OT and Apocrypha (2 Mac. 4:37; 3 Mac. 4:4; 3 Mac. 6:23; 4 Mac. 15:20; Job 3:24; Sir. 12:16; Sir. 31:13; Mic. 2:6; Ezek. 27:35). Do you think this is significant or not?

Verse 36 gets at the most important point: Jesus' emotion is generated by his love (*phileō*). I have found that many people try to derive a distinction between the kind of love God has for us, which they refer to as *agape* (verb *agapaō*), and the kind of "lower-order" love people have for each other (*phileō*); John obliterates any such notion. The divine/human dichotomy or dualism that many of us insist upon is not tolerated by the Jesus in John. That's part of the point of the incarnation—to help us to stop imagining God and Jesus as "up there" in some ethereal realm that is untainted by humanity, while "down here" is the mundane, profane world unfit to host God—as if it were *our* house. But more on that when we study John 14 and 21. If you do a study, you will see that both verbs are used both for humans and for God and Jesus.

2. Francis J. Moloney, *The Gospel of John*, Sacra Pagina 4 (Collegeville, MN: The Liturgical Press, 1998), 330.

Jesus comes to the tomb in verse 38. The word "tomb" (Gk. *mnēmeion*) occurs fourteen times in John. Surely the author expects us to recall 5:28, where Jesus says: "Do not be astonished at this; for the hour is coming when all who are in their tombs [NRSV "graves"] will hear his voice." The next time we see the word, Jesus is calling out to Lazarus in a loud voice to "come out." The next occurrence after that is Jesus' own tomb (20:1), where another stone (*lithos*) appears, and is taken away, just as it is here in verse 39.

Now the attention turns back to Martha. She emphasizes how dead Lazarus is with the comment about the stench. It is in no way accidental that, right after this passage, Mary, the sister of Lazarus (remember: *not* a "sinner" as in Luke 7 and *not* Mary Magdalene and *not* a prostitute) will anoint Jesus' feet as a furtherance of the foreshadowing of his death here in chapter 11 and will amply overturn the stench. At 12:3 we learn that "the house was filled with the fragrance of the perfume." Can you smell the stench of death in any of its forms—death of a relationship, a dream, an ability, a loved one? Can you smell the fragrance of hope and redemption and new life, or at least begin to imagine what it would smell like?

Standing by the tomb, Jesus prays. His trust in God's glory and faithfulness and ability to restore life is unequivocal—not so for the bystanders. So he prays for their benefit (11:41–42; notice how similar his prayer here is to the one he prays at 12:27–30), and, true to his prophecy in chapters 5 and 10, he calls his sheep by name, and they come out of the places of dank death. Verse 44 tells us that the "dead man came out." But the dead man is still bound. Notice what Jesus does. He does not personally zap away the trappings by fiat; rather, he calls the *community* to unbind the man who had been held captive by the dank stench of death.

This powerful point was made real to me for the first time one semester when I taught a seminar on John, as I am wont to do. For the creative project, one student (now the Rev. Lynette Ross), a member of the LGBTQ community, wrote and embodied a "Coming Out" liturgy based on the Lazarus story. In response to Jesus' command, the rest of the class participated in the removal of the bindings. I study and write on John for a living, but I had never thought about the fact that although Jesus started the process, the *community* was enjoined to participate in and complete the unbinding of the person formerly imprisoned and isolated in a tomb. If Jesus is about life, then surely the community should be as well, here and now—not in some utopian future that almost enervated Martha back at verse 24. Rev. Ross's work has obvious implications for congregations with LGBTQ commitments, but I think it applies much more generally as well. Don't you?

Lazarus

While Martha may be the weightiest character in chapter 11, Lazarus exerts his literary power by virtue of his silence and lack of specific personality. His lack of definition as a character makes ample room for the reader to fill in the story, spark the imagination, and ask some important questions.

For example, what kills Lazarus? The use of the imperfect verb tense in verse 1 might imply that Lazarus has a chronic illness or disability. The onlookers ask the poignant, perennial question that arises for persons with disabilities and those who love them: "Could not he who opened the eyes of the blind man have kept this man from dying?" (v. 37). The reader already knows that the simple answer to that is yes, based on the healing story in chapter 4. But this is not that story.

Second, I mentioned the importance of the community above, but I wonder further about the community's behavior before this scene. Communities disable and enable. Throughout the chapter the whole community has gathered around to fret and mourn dramatically for a few days. But does the community have the will to enable Lazarus, not just in those first dramatic moments, but for the rest of his life? The miraculous healing symbolically makes the christological point that Jesus, like God, is in the glorious business of life. But the physical cure itself is evanescent, since Lazarus will die again at some point.

The story is about Jesus, but the story is, more importantly, about what kind of communities we create: Are they disabling or enabling? Jesus cures the impairment, but the community has the power to remove the disability/bindings. And could it be that Jesus is actually upset because while flamboyant theatrics and (feigned?) concern arise once the disabled Lazarus is dead, one wonders whether the level of energy and concern were there before he died (and did the lack of it speed his death?), and will it be there once he is among them again?

Third, I wonder about the reaction of the religious authorities. As in chapters 5 and 9, the healing of Lazarus does not cause the authorities to celebrate or give glory to God. Rather, "the chief priests planned to put Lazarus to death as well, since it was on account of him that many of the Jews were deserting and were believing in Jesus" (12:10–11). Certain social, political, economic, and religious systems benefit from keeping some people disabled or dead. The raising of Lazarus serves to foreshadow Jesus' own death and resurrection. Jesus dies only once, of course. Lazarus will eventually die again, but that will not be ultimately devastating. John assures us that once one grasps the ultimate, eternal power of the resurrection and the life available through Jesus, and the fact that both start here and now, the grave can offer no real threat. Only three chapters later Jesus will reiterate the point by announcing, "I am the way; that is, the truth and the life" (my trans.). Indeed, he is!

Promises and Pitfalls

From a disability perspective, the story has liberative potential. It calls readers to stop playing the "if only" game, to embrace abundant life in the present, and to enjoy the peace that Christ brings even in the face of suffering and death. It challenges society to understand that both disability and liberation are a communal project, not an individual's problem that the person should figure out how to solve. Many would like to take the approach of Pontius Pilate, whereby they wash their hands of the whole matter. Alas, Pontius Pilate is not a strong role model.

But the text may leave us unsatisfied in other ways. First, Lazarus never gets to speak anywhere in the Gospel. He has no agency but appears only as an object to be discussed and acted upon. It is another example of narrative prosthesis, in which Lazarus is more of a device to convey the Gospel's Christology than a character in his own right. Second, the theodicy question (the defense of God's love and justice in light of evil, suffering, and death) will still burn in the hearts of many: "Could not he who opened the eyes of the blind man have kept this man from dying?" (11:37). And why are some cured and others not? Third, the notion that Jesus intentionally allowed Lazarus to die in order to allow God to perform a publicity stunt to get more adherents (as the text seems to indicate at vv. 4, 15, and 40–42) remains problematic for some readers.

Conclusion

If anyone has reason to tackle the Lazarus story from all angles, it's me. When I was around seven or eight, my parents sent me to Vacation Bible School (VBS) somewhere to get me out of their hair for a bit (or maybe get me spiritually formed). At one point at VBS we all sat in a circle waiting in suspense for someone to arrive. When we could hardly stand it anymore, the door opened and a stretcher was wheeled in. On it lay a very large man (I was seven, so at least he seemed large) wrapped like a mummy. As I watched in terror, the giant man got up (he seemed even bigger then) and started walking in our direction like a mummy (because I'd seen lots of Scooby Doo, I knew how mummies walked). It was terrifying!

That is my enduring image of that VBS. I'm sure at some point some adult was explaining to me how all of this was "good news" and that I should become a Christian to hear more about it. I have no recollection of the narrative, just the visual. I will say that when I got off at my bus stop later that day, they gave me a kite. I don't know if it made up for the trauma, but that seemed a little closer to "good news"!

Well, eventually I did become a Christian. Four decades after that VBS lesson, I find that I spend much of my time studying, writing, and speaking on this very story! I'll let you decide if I'm just still trying to work through the childhood experience or if it was a crucial moment in the shaping of my call—or just a funny story. Or all of the above. One thing is for sure: what you do in VBS can shape a person for life!

Chapter 8

Footwashing Feats: Mary of Bethany and Jesus of Nazareth

John 12 and 13

Loving by Serving: Feetwiping Part 1 (John 12)

Read John 12:1–8. Think of someone you know (it may be you!) who comes to mind when you hear the word "hospitality." What makes that person your go-to example? How does that person make you feel?

How should we define hospitality? Maybe it's one of those things that's hard to define but you know it when you see it, and you know when it's absent. Hospitality, in its truest form, is opening ourselves to another person in mutual reverence. It means seeing God in each and every person we meet in passing or live with day in and day out. Hospitality, above all else, is about being in *mutual relationship*, however briefly, with another person.

Martha and Mary model Christian hospitality. Jesus, the Lamb who takes away the sin of the world, has come from Galilee and is heading to Jerusalem to die in place of the sacrificial Passover lamb. It is no accident, then, that the author tells us that it is six days before Passover. Jesus stops by the home of Lazarus, whose resurrection occurred in the previous chapter (remember, the author expects you to be reading this all the way through, in order, uninterrupted). John tells us that Jesus is particularly close to this family in Bethany. The siblings host a dinner for Jesus. Martha provides food, a basic physical necessity.

Then Mary makes her memorable move. She takes an abundant amount of expensive perfume (about twelve ounces) and anoints Jesus' feet with it. Not his head—his feet. Picture yourself in that position. While it was customary to anoint the head of a king or even other people, to anoint the feet was an act of tender devotion. What's more, she uses her own clearly uncovered hair to wipe his feet. Notice that she is not a "sinner" (i.e., don't confuse her with the woman in Luke 7:36–50); she is not a prostitute; and she is not Mary Magdalene.

What features of hospitality stand out so far? First, it's important to attend to the basic physical needs of a person.

Second, clearly a number of people were there. Hospitality says, "The more the merrier."

Third, Mary doesn't just respond to a need that is expressed; she actually *anticipates* Jesus' need, as is indicated by Jesus' words in verse 7: "Leave her alone. She bought it so that she might keep it for the day of my burial." She foreshadows what Jesus does in the footwashing, where he anticipates the needs of his followers. Here's what I mean: the word "wipe" (*ekmassō*) occurs elsewhere only when Jesus wipes the disciples' feet at 13:5, as he tells them to do the same for others. She does it before Jesus even teaches it!

John has a way of tagging characters with recurring descriptors. For example, Nicodemus is repeatedly referred to as the one who came to Jesus "by night." Lazarus is referred to as "the one Jesus raised from the dead." And Mary? Well, in 11:2, before she even does the anointing, the King James Version refers to her in this way: "(It was *that* Mary which anointed the Lord with ointment, and wiped his feet with her hair, whose brother Lazarus was sick.)"

Fourth, this is an intimate, touchy Gospel. Bodies matter. Hospitality and real bodies, with all of the attendant smells, go hand in hand.

Fifth, Mary gives from what she has at that moment, without worrying that it's not good enough and without waiting for a so-called "more opportune" time. The nard is certainly nice, but what matters most is that she gives of herself. She opens herself up and makes herself vulnerable and available to another person at the risk of being rejected, criticized, or ridiculed for her action—by someone like Judas.

Mary vs. Judas

We have already seen that John likes to play characters off of one another for effect; I have called it intercharacterization. We saw it with

Nicodemus and the Samaritan woman; the disciples and the Samaritan woman; the man in chapter 5 and the man in chapter 9. Now we see Judas contrasted with Mary. Let me warn you—this author really has no tender feelings for Judas. Judas is mentioned nine times, and the author almost always includes a dig of some sort. He is tagged most commonly as the betrayer and sometimes as a thief. You would do well to compare the character of Judas in the Fourth Gospel with his appearance in the Synoptics (to see the interesting variety at play), but such is not our task here. He first appears in 6:64, 70–71: "'But among you there are some who do not believe.' For Jesus knew from the first who were the ones that did not believe, and who was the one that would betray him. . . . Jesus answered them, 'Did I not choose you, the twelve? Yet one of you is a devil.' He was speaking of Judas son of Simon Iscariot, for he, though one of the twelve, was going to betray him." He appears further at John 13:2, 26, 29; 18:2–5.

In John 12, right in the midst of Mary's gracious, selfless, generous, daring act of hospitality, Judas tries to kill the moment. One can imagine the mystical moment, marked by the rare redolent smell of such evanescent luxuriousness—the smell that takes you away to another place, lifts you, elevates you, pampers you, renews you. Everyone is enjoying the gift—well, almost everyone. Into the mix, Judas brings his joy-robbing, cynicism-disguised-as-realism, selfishness-disguised-as-altruism self.

What exactly makes Judas the bad example of discipleship in contrast to Mary's good example? Here are some of my ideas. I expect you to add yours. Extending hospitality costs Mary dearly, but it gives life to another. In this way she acts in keeping with Christ's crucifixion. Mary represents life givers; Judas represents life robbers. This act of hospitality costs Mary dearly, yet she doesn't count the cost; it costs Judas nothing, yet he's all noisy concern. But the text makes us ask ourselves a hard question. When we pull the "this isn't practical" or "this isn't good stewardship" card, are we really worried about bad stewardship, or are we balking at getting involved in something that could cost us personally? The text makes it clear that Judas hid behind the "good stewardship" excuse to mask his own tendency toward life robbing. He didn't care about the poor; he just didn't like the implications of radical hospitality and what it might cost him personally.

Do you sometimes find in your community that those who complain the loudest and most bitterly are those who give the least of themselves? Maybe we've been that person. Anyway, Judas stands as a stark warning.

And another contrast: Mary's single act is direct, immediate service to another person here and now—not some vague, theoretical, future-oriented deal (whereas Judas invokes a theoretical concern that he never is seen actually living out). She doesn't wait to act until there is a "program" in place.

Like Jesus, and unlike Judas, Mary operates from a *theology of abundance* rather than a theology of scarcity. Life is not a zero-sum game. There's more than enough for everyone, as Mary would recall from the story of Elijah and the oil (1 Kgs. 17:8–16), Psalm 23, the manna in the wilderness (Exod. 16:4–36), the Hanukah story (1 and 2 Maccabees), and so on. This is God we are talking about, after all—not Zeus or some such, but the God of Abraham and Sarah, Rebekah and Isaac, Jacob and Rachel and Leah. God: our Creator, Redeemer, and Sustainer.

Biblical hospitality tends toward extravagance and abundance. The point is emphasized: it's costly, pure, and so abundant that the entire room is redolent of it. It costs financially, and it costs personally. Radical acts of hospitality make you vulnerable to attack by the "practical" folks. God's hospitality is no more practical than God's grace. Judas suffers from the same malady as the prodigal son's older brother and the prophet Jonah—and maybe us. Is extravagance good stewardship, we ask? Should we spend $10,000 on carpeting or a baptistry when we could use it for something more practical like the food bank? Extravagance, abundance. "I came that they might have *life*, and have it *abundantly*" (10:10).

Think of things in your home or your church that send miserly signals instead of celebratory welcome signals. I once belonged to a church that routinely didn't print enough bulletins or put out enough chairs. It sent an awful signal. Sometimes at my home there are arguments about how much food to purchase and put out at a party. What does hospitality require?

What's the difference between extravagant and wasteful? Aren't we called at times, in the name of hospitality and community building and gospel sharing, to be prodigal? Have you ever seen the movie *Babette's Feast*? If not, I encourage you to do so as you contemplate this passage, Christian hospitality, and the nature of the gospel.

Mary's act of hospitality is deeply theological. Jesus says, "She bought it so that she might keep it for the day of my burial." All Christian hospitality is rooted in God's welcome as it has been expressed through the life, death, and resurrection of Jesus Christ. We welcome others because God first welcomed us. We're not in the business of just being nice people. We extend hospitality as a sign of the presence in our world of the risen Christ, who longs to gather into one the dispersed people of God—that is, all people. So every act of hospitality at every point in our lives should be clearly rooted in the gospel. "Practice random acts of kindness and senseless beauty" sounds beautiful, but it isn't Christian. Our hospitality isn't random or senseless; it's anchored firmly and quite intentionally to the cross and resurrection of Jesus Christ.

Finally, Mary's act of hospitality is conducted in her home with someone she is intimately connected with. Frankly, this part strikes me very seriously. How hospitable am I to those closest to me? Do I treat them with all or any of the characteristics mentioned above? Have you ever noticed yourself being, as one writer puts it, a "quivering mass of availability" to numerous complete strangers but barely present to your own friends and family? Has your partner or spouse ever asked you, gently and fairly, or not so gently but still fairly, "Could you just arrange your schedule such that we don't have to get the dregs, the leftovers?"

I love conversations and programs that help us generate practical ideas and programs that exude hospitality, but I wonder if we can also practice being present and hospitable to those whom God has placed in our path already. In other words, can we become more hospitable people before worrying extensively about creating more hospitable programs? What would it look like for us to practice the hospitable traits exhibited by Mary toward those closest to us? They are no less "the other" in our lives for whom Christ died and rose again so that abundant life might be the norm.

On to Jerusalem

Word gets out that Jesus is back in Bethany (after raising Lazarus, he had gone to Ephraim [11:54]). Recall that there is a warrant out for his arrest (11:57), since the religious authorities are upset that so many people of their flock are following Jesus (11:48; 12:11). They decide not only to kill Jesus, but to kill Lazarus as well. Isn't it true that sometimes we would rather see a person stay dead if their resurrection to new life requires us to see the world, our neighbors, and ourselves in a new way? Isn't the status quo convenient in some ways? Do we love convenience and expedience more than Truth and Life?

Jesus enters Jerusalem as the King of Israel, a point made clear by the Pharisees' exasperated statement: "You see, you can do nothing. Look, the world has gone after him!" (12:19). But remember 10:16, where Jesus says, "I have other sheep that do not belong to this fold. I must bring them also, and they will listen to my voice. So there will be one flock, one shepherd"? Well, here they are. Having established himself as the Shepherd of Israel, now he turns to the Greeks. Once Jesus hears the news of their seeking him, he knows his "hour" has arrived, that his work is nearly done. He then predicts his own passion: "Very truly, I tell you, unless a grain of wheat falls into the earth and dies, it remains just a single grain; but if it dies, it bears much fruit. Those who love their life lose it, and those who hate their life in this world will keep it for eternal life" (12:24–25). In this Gospel, Jesus knows what he has come to do and never questions that work.

In the Synoptic Gospels, Jesus asks that the cup pass from him (in Luke he even sweats blood). Not so in John; in fact, Jesus dismisses the very idea of it as ridiculous: "and what should I say—'Father, save me from this hour'? No, it is for this reason that I have come to this hour" (12:27). Instead, Jesus prays for God to glorify God's name. In John there is never any perceived disconnect between Jesus and God (which is why John does not record a cry of dereliction from the cross), so God immediately responds to Jesus for the sake of the crowd (not for Jesus' sake, since Jesus is already perfectly united with God's will in every way). Jesus boldly and crucially declares: "And I, when I am lifted up from the earth [i.e., crucifixion], will draw *all people* to myself" (12:32). And why would he not? After all, we know from chapter 1 that all things came into being through him and he is the light of *all people*, and from 4:42 that he is the Savior not only of Jews and Samaritans, but of the whole cosmos!

Just as John begins the Gospel by depicting Jesus as Lady

Wisdom, so too he concludes the Book of Signs with Jesus, like Lady Wisdom, crying aloud (12:44), announcing the gospel one last time before turning inward to his disciples and preparing them for his physical departure (12:44–50). If you reread 3:17–21, you will see that he is quoting himself: "I have come as light into the world, so that everyone who believes in me should not remain in the darkness. I do not judge anyone who hears my words and does not keep them, for I came not to judge the world, but to save the world" (12:46–47).

Saving by Serving: Feetwiping Part 2 (John 13)

In chapters 13–17 Jesus equips his uncomprehending disciples (and us) to continue his ministry in the world after he physically departs. Thus we call this section of John the Farewell Discourse. Chapter 13 begins and ends with love. In one of the most poignant statements in the Bible, John says, "Having loved his own who were in the world, he loved them to the end" (v. 1b). Indeed. Did then and does now. Jesus loves the disciples fully, even though he knows everything about them, including the fact that one is going to betray him and one deny. This does not stop him from demonstrating that love takes form in service—even to his momentary or permanent enemies.

Feet, the act of wiping, food, and Judas connect this chapter tightly with chapter 12. Once again we find Jesus at a meal with those whom he loves (cf. 12:1–8), including Judas. In the course of this meal, he stands and washes the feet of all of them (recall the symbolic importance of water in this Gospel). Like Mary, he attends to the care of their bodies in intimate, touchy ways; like her, he wipes (*ekmassō*) their feet. Have you ever performed or received a footwashing in community? Obviously, this is a very intimate act. Furthermore, a servant, not the host, usually performed footwashing. Here Jesus models a very different way of being in community: the use of power in the service of love; getting involved in an up close and personal way; creating spaces for trust and vulnerability to form. He does this even when it is highly likely, if not certain, that at least one person in the group will turn out not to be so trustworthy or other-oriented, will take but not give, will attempt to control rather than serve the community and its leaders.

Speaking of leadership, notice how democratic and egalitarian the model is here. At no point in John is Peter (or anyone else, for that matter) given the keys to the kingdom (cf. Matt. 18) and told that the church will be built upon him. As we noted in chapter 1, the main disciple, the Beloved Disciple, is never even named in the Gospel. The Gospel of John challenges our notions of power and leadership in profound ways. In fact, as we will see in chapter 15, this Gospel declares us to be "friends" of Jesus.

Judas usually piques people's curiosity. John indicates that Satan (also called "the ruler of this world" in John) directs Judas's actions. Some people blame Judas and fear that "the devil made me do it" attitude may keep a person from taking responsibility for choices freely made. Others feel sorry for Judas and see him as a pawn in a cosmic battle beyond his comprehension or an actor who must adhere to the script that he has been given by the Producer (that is, God). What do you think about him? You might argue that he is a more sympathetic character in the Synoptic Gospels. It is surely no accident that John seals Judas's exit here with the phrase "And it was night." Recall 3:19–20: "And this is the judgment, that the light has come into the world, and people loved darkness rather than light because their deeds were evil. For all who do evil hate the light and do not come to the light, so that their deeds may not be exposed."

Again Jesus indicates that he is about to leave them and that, for now, they cannot follow. Only he can accomplish this particular task, and he will do it by himself (in fact, in John, Jesus even carries his own cross, whereas in the Synoptics, Simon of Cyrene helps him). He then gives them a single commandment: "Just as I have loved you, you also should love one another. By this everyone will know that you are my disciples, if you have love for one another" (13:34–35). Having shown them what love looks like in practice, he announces that there will be only one standard for identifying a Christian: it's not purity, or Bible knowledge, or holiness—it's love (see 15:9–17). John uses a number of different words for love and uses them frequently. This Gospel is obsessed with love. Are we?

In the Synoptic Gospels, Jesus eats a Passover meal with his disciples and delivers the Words of Institution that Christians typically hear before they receive the Lord's Supper/Communion/Eucharist; then Peter's betrayal is foretold (Mark 14; Matt. 26; Luke 22). This event is usually called the Last Supper. While this meal in John 13 is Jesus' last preresurrection meal with the disciples, there are no Words of Institution, and it is not a Passover meal. In fact, by the time the disciples are having the Last Supper with Jesus in the Synoptics, Jesus is already dead in John. In John, he dies at the time that the Passover lamb is slaughtered. Do you see the symbolism? Many people find in John 6:22–59 a kind of parallel to the Synoptics' Words of Institution. John loves symbols and metaphor. You may find it worthwhile to note the similarities and differences between John and the Synoptics—not in order to "fix" one or the other but to get clear in your mind how each separate author tells the story. We have four different Gospels for a reason.[1]

One crucial difference is the presence of the Beloved Disciple at this meal with Jesus. He reclines upon Jesus' breast (*kolpos*), a very intimate posture. In fact it's the same kind of nestling that we see between Jesus and God in 1:18 (*kolpos*). This unusual word occurs in John only in these two places—it's not at all accidental. The KJV and NASB translate correctly here "leaning/reclining *on* Jesus' bosom/breast" (13:23), whereas the NRSV incorrectly and inexplicably moves the Beloved Disciple *next to* Jesus. We are supposed to identify with the unnamed Beloved Disciple. What is it like for you to imagine leaning on Jesus' breast? I wonder if we really understand the level of tenderness God has for each of us, or whether it's too uncomfortable or embarrassing to embrace. If so, I wonder why. If not, can we find a way to live with that knowledge and feeling close at hand even more often?

As for Peter, he is far too distracted by his anxiety around Jesus' ominous words about leaving to hear Jesus' love command. He does not understand about the cross. And he does not yet understand the terrain of the human heart, including his, and its capacity to disappoint when it perceives danger to the self. Peter means wholeheartedly what he is saying. And in the end he will, in fact, follow Jesus unto death for the sake of the gospel. Redemption always has the last word. But not before struggling mightily with a very public, shame-filled failure. In fact, isn't that a crucial component of any powerful

1. For more on this, see "Four Gospels: Problem or Gift?" in Clark-Soles, *Engaging the Word* (Louisville, KY: Westminster John Knox Press, 2010), 35–54.

redemption story? If you have never surprised yourself with a painful moral failure, I am unlikely to seek you out as a trusted spiritual mentor.

Watching Jesus follow his calling with intention throughout and root Peter on as he slowly discerns his own call and struggles to fulfill it makes me think about my own calling. What about yours? Some of us know what we were born to do from the start and do not waver much. Others of us figure it out in fits and starts. Notice that Peter wants to follow Jesus *now*, which is admirable in its own way. But sometimes our passion must give way to patience. We have to distinguish the gift of *now* from the tyranny of *now*. The Gospel of John artfully does a both/and here. On the one hand, now is full of the presence of God and eternal life; we don't have to wait for the sweet by-and-by in order to seize the day, the love, joy, and peace promised by Jesus. But sometimes we have to be satisfied with being pointed in the right direction by signs and have faith that the fuller truth will unfold. You see, the disciples cannot have the necessary knowledge until the rest of the story unfolds—until he is crucified and raised and bestows the Spirit upon them. Maybe you are more like Peter than Jesus in this way. If you are struggling or just waiting, this Gospel tells us that such holy work is best done in community.

If chapter 13 ends with Peter hearing a difficult truth about himself that he cannot yet grasp, chapter 14 turns immediately to consolation.

> ***Prayer:*** *God, teach us to love one another as you have loved us; that is, not in an ethereal, heady, abstract way, but in a way that bends down to scrub dirty feet with hands and maybe even wipe them with our hair. Amen.*

Chapter 9

There's No Place like Home

John 14

The Farewell Discourse falls into the genre of testamentary literature (as in last will and testament). Recall the patriarchs on their deathbeds, bequeathing belongings and wisdom to their progeny (e.g., Isaac in Gen. 27 and Jacob in Gen. 48). Jesus has no material goods to dispense; instead he gives his disciples peace (14:27) and the power to do even greater works than he himself did during his earthly sojourn (14:12).

John 14:1 says: "Let the heart of y'all not be troubled" (my trans.). Using the second-person plural (y'all), Jesus moves from personal conversation with one disciple (Peter, 13:36–38) to address the whole group: "Let y'all's heart not be troubled." Notice, though, that they share only *one* heart: "Let not your (plural) heart (singular) be troubled" (the NRSV misleads here by saying "hearts" instead of heart). Like it or not, John insists that we are all in this together. The same sentence appears at verse 27, forming a contained unit: "Let y'all's heart not be troubled."

Why would their collective heart be troubled? Because, despite having heard Jesus repeatedly indicate that he was going to be lifted up on the cross (3:14; 8:28; 12:32), the disciples cannot imagine life on earth without the earthly Jesus. They cannot, for the life of them or by the death of him, see how his departure could be good in any way. So Jesus says what he always does: "Trust me." Believe or trust language (*pisteuō*) occurs ninety-eight times in John, always as a verb, never as a noun. Trusting is a dynamic process.

Not only do the disciples share *one* heart but also *one* home (*oikia*), God's home. House and home language occur frequently and significantly in this Gospel. John routinely invokes the language of home, of family, of radical intimacy. In fact, every relationship humans consider primary is alluded to: parent (2:3); partner (4:16); bride, groom, and friend of the bridegroom (3:29); sibling (11:1); friend (15:15); child (8:35); and teacher (13:13). There is *one* house.

The one house, however, has many "dwelling places," which is not surprising, since we have heard from the beginning that Jesus is the Savior of the whole cosmos (Gk. *kosmos*, 4:42) that he helped to create (1:9) and that his crucifixion is all-inclusive: "And I, when I am lifted up from the earth, will draw *all* people to myself" (12:32). All (*pas*), not some; that's a lot of people, requiring many "abiding places" (*monai*). *Monai* is a noun from the verb *menō*, "abide," which is one of John's favorite words (used thirty-seven times, most famously in the vine-and-branches speech of chap. 15). Throughout the Gospel, John invites the reader to abide with Jesus and therefore have life, eternal life, true life, which begins now (20:31). John 14:23 reads, "Those who love me will keep my word, and my Father will love them, and we will come to them and make our abiding place (*monē*) with them" (my trans.).

Jesus prepares this "place" (*topos*) where we are all united in God's household by heading to the cross. There he births the church, God's home: "Then he said to the disciple, 'Here is your mother.' And from that hour the disciple took her into his own home" (19:27). After all, home is where the (singular) heart is. Church is a real place (*topos*), not a u-topia (from Gk. *ou* "not" + *topos* "place"). Augustine proclaimed: "Our heart is restless until it finds rest in thee."[1] Church is to be such a place.

Jesus comes and goes often in John. From the start, we know Jesus as "the one coming into the world" (1:9). His departure only serves the goal of his eternal return whereby, thanks to the Paraclete (one of John's names for the Holy Spirit), we will enjoy immediate, full, eternal unity with Jesus and, therefore, God.

Enter Thomas, the Eeyore of the Fourth Gospel, who first appears at 11:16 and who assumes the practical (veering toward the pessimistic) role and asks a fair question. On the heels of Jesus' grandiloquent

1. *Soliloquies* I.i.3 in *Augustine: Earlier Writings,* ed. J. H. S. Burleigh (London: SCM, 1953), 23.

locution about abiding places and enigmatic travel plans, Thomas, in a voice somewhat weary but not yet despairing, cuts to the chase: "We actually *don't* know and, frankly we don't even know *how* to know" (14:5, my paraphrase). How often do Jesus' disciples plead either total or partial ignorance, such that they are excused from decision making or action? They are looking for seven habits, nine steps, or ten commandments when the answer lies in intimate, if confusing and challenging, relationships—the preeminent one being between Jesus and them. Jesus, for his part, is having none of it: "You know enough because you know me" (v. 7, my trans.). Train your eyes on me, and the path will always be true and life-giving. "I am the Way; that is, the truth and the life" (v. 6, my trans.). Here the words "truth" and "life" further describe the meaning of the Way rather than introduce two more separate features of Jesus (known as the "epexegetical *kai*" in Gk. grammar).

John 14:6 may raise questions about Christian exclusivism. Contemporary interpreters should be cautioned to attend first to the original context before moving to our own. First, John repeatedly insists on the universal scope of Christ's work (1:9; 4:42; 12:32). At 10:16 Jesus declares, somewhat enigmatically, that he has "other sheep that do not belong to *this* fold." To some, John is the most universalistic of the Gospels. To others, who contend that the original first-century Johannine community was forged in stressful, sectarian circumstances that led John to think in binary, exclusive, oppositional categories, John is the most sectarian of the Gospels.

Second, those who see in 14:6 a verse to use to convince unbelievers that they had better become Christian or suffer eternal exclusion from the kingdom of God should note that the Farewell Discourse is addressed to those who are *already* Christian, encouraging them to drop the excuses for inefficacy and, instead, trust that we know enough and are equipped enough to do greater works than Jesus himself did. Jesus draws all to God. He does this in an endless variety of ways, some that we can name based on our knowledge and experience and some that must remain a mystery for us created, finite beings.

Where Thomas lamented lack of knowledge, Philip now demonstrates lack of insight and vision. Unlike the Synoptic Gospels, the Gospel of John considers Philip a main character; he is named twelve times, as opposed to three in Matthew and Mark and two in Luke. He appears at the beginning of Jesus' ministry; after the brothers Andrew and Peter, who were also from Bethsaida, Philip is the next one to follow. He is the first disciple to lead someone else (Nathanael) to Jesus and the first disciple to make a proclamation about Jesus: "We have found him about whom Moses in the law and also the prophets wrote" (1:45). That encounter ends with Jesus announcing that he has, in effect, replaced Jacob's ladder (1:51). In chapter 6, Jesus "tests" Philip about feeding the crowds; Philip cannot see his way to the grandiosity of Jesus' works, but the work occurs anyway. Philip also participates in the crucial turning point in the Gospel: when the Greeks arrive, they first consult Philip. After Philip (and Andrew) informs him about this development, Jesus declares: "The hour has come for the Son of Man to be glorified" (12:23). Presumably Philip remains on the scene to witness the exchange between Jesus and God (12:27–28).

While Thomas speaks as a representative of the group and Jesus answers him as such (using second-person-plural verbs), when Philip tries the same move, Jesus gets personal with him: "Have I been with y'all (plural) all this time, Philip, and you (singular) still do not know me? . . . How can you (singular) say, 'Show us the Father?'" (14:9, my trans.). Philip presses Jesus for more, so that the disciples might be "satisfied" (*arkeō*). This is important: the only other occurrence of this word appears in Jesus' exchange with Philip about feeding the crowd. There Philip again protests that what is available is not sufficient or satisfactory (*arkeō*, 6:7) to complete God's work. Philip operates from a theology of scarcity as he stares blindly into the face of the Good Shepherd who makes our cup overflow (Ps. 23:5) and who came that we might have life and have it more abundantly (10:10). Philip demands "satisfaction," while Jesus is longing to gift him beyond measure.

How should Philip (and we) know that Jesus and God are unified? By attending to Jesus' words and works: "The words that I say to you I do not speak on my own; but the Father who dwells (*menō*) in me does his works" (14:10). Words and works are not two separate things for John, because—even as *we* know on our best days—words *are* works. Jesus' words are both authoritative and effective. His words are at least as authoritative as Scripture (2:22), if not more so (5:39–47). Like Scripture, Jesus' words are said to be fulfilled and are to be kept and observed and believed. Jesus speaks efficaciously. At 4:50–51, he heals by a word, from a distance: "Jesus said to him [the royal official], 'Go; your son will live.' The man believed the word that Jesus spoke to him and started on his way. As he was going down, his slaves met him and told him that his child was alive." At 5:8–9, "Jesus said . . . , 'Stand up, take your mat and walk.' At once the man was made well, and he took up his mat and began to walk."

The language of works (*ergon,* "work"; we get the word "ergonomic" from this) appears heavily in the Gospel, not to mention verbs of doing (*poieō*; we get the word "poem" from this) and the occurrences of signs. The Father works and Jesus works, indistinguishably and vitally: "The Father loves the Son and shows him all that he himself is doing; he will show him [even] greater works than these (*kai meizona toutōn*), so that you will be astonished" (5:20). Note how 14:12 parallels 5:20, using the exact same language. That is, as impressive as it may be for Jesus to do the very works of God, even more captivating is Jesus' claim that whoever trusts in Jesus will also do the very works that Jesus and God do.

Further, the one who trusts will do even *greater* works than these (*kai meizona toutōn*). Astonishing indeed. Christians can do what Jesus did and more, and many have over these two thousand years (from the mundane to the miraculous). Whether we *will* do them is up to us; the fact that we *can* do them is due to the fact that Jesus completed the very work God sent him to do (19:30), such that if we ask *anything* in the name of Jesus, he will do it. Jesus appears to have left no room for his disciples to dream small.

In 14:15–17, Jesus reiterates his favorite theme (love), promises the Holy Spirit, and emphasizes the intimate unity of Jesus, God, the Spirit, and the believer. John uses love verbs (*agapaō, phileō*) fifty-seven times, compared to Matthew's thirteen, Mark's six, and Luke's fifteen. The noun love (*agapē*) is used seven times; Matthew and Luke only use it once and Mark never. Friend (*philos*) appears six times in John, while Matthew uses it once, Mark never, and Luke fifteen times. Unlike John, where *philos* is a word Jesus uses about his own real followers, Luke's Jesus uses it primarily in parables. And remember that the primary disciple in John is named only as the Beloved Disciple. Given the overwhelming prevalence of love language in the Fourth Gospel, we might accuse the author of preoccupation with a single issue. And why not? "For God so loved the world that he gave his only Son, so that everyone who believes in him may not perish but may have eternal life" (3:16).

In verse 15 Jesus declares that if his disciples love him, they will keep his commandments. The reader may ask, "What commandments?" Unlike Matthew, nowhere in John does Jesus command us to go the second mile, turn the other cheek, or render unto Caesar that which is Caesar's. Famously, Jesus issues a single commandment in John: "I give you a new commandment, that you love one another. Just as I have loved you, you also should love one another. By this everyone will know that you are my disciples, if you have love for one another" (13:34–35). Furthermore, he reiterates this in the chapter immediately succeeding ours: "This is my commandment, that you love one another as I have loved you. No one has greater love than this, to lay down one's life for one's friends" (15:12–13). William Sloane Coffin had it right when he said, "If we fail in love, we fail in all things else."

Please resist the common but mistaken urge to distinguish between God's way of loving (*agapaō, agapē*) and human ways of loving (*phileō, philos*), with the former considered to be superior to the latter. The Gospel of John makes the *exact opposite* move, in fact. The Gospel uses the language interchangeably for both God and people. God loves Jesus (5:20); God loves the followers (16:27); Jesus loves his followers (20:2); the followers love Jesus (16:27), and so on—using both *phileō* and *agapaō*. This is a major theological claim for John: the so-called dividing line between divine and human love simply does not exist. Should this be surprising in a Gospel that insists so radically upon the incarnation?

The Holy Spirit

Admittedly, John's ideas about the Holy Spirit are somewhat unusual compared to other New Testament texts. All of the Gospels refer to the Holy Spirit descending upon Jesus like a dove. However, in contrast to Luke, who depicts the Holy Spirit as heavily active in the lives of characters from the beginning of his Gospel until the end of Acts, John insists that the Holy Spirit will become active for believers only after Jesus himself departs ("Now he said this about the Spirit, which believers in him were to receive; for as yet there was no Spirit, because Jesus was not yet glorified," 7:39).

Why is this? A clue lies in Jesus' referring to the Holy Spirit not as *the* Paraclete but rather as *another* (*allon*) Paraclete (14:16). Jesus is the first; for the Spirit to be active among them while Jesus is there would be redundant, since they each serve the same revelatory function. What appears to be bad news to the disciples, namely, Jesus' departure from them, turns out to be the best of news for both them and us. While Jesus walks the earth, his ministry is limited to one locale and one person, himself. Upon his departure, his disciples are given the Spirit and graduate from apprentices to full, mature revealers of God's love. The same holds true for all future disciples who never encounter the historical Jesus; contemporary believers have no disadvantage in comparison to the first believers. Everything that the first believers are taught and experience is available to us to the same degree and with equally rich texture.

The word *paraklētos* presents notorious translation difficulty, because it has a range of meanings in the Greek, all of which the author signifies. English translations variously translate it "Comforter," "Advocate," "Counselor," and "Helper"; it might be best to keep it in its transliterated form, Paraclete, so as to catch the attention of the hearer with the strangeness. After all, it is strange among biblical authors too. It appears only five times in the New Testament: four times in the Farewell Discourse (14:16, 26; 15:26; 16:7) and once in 1 John 2:1. Narrowing the Greek word to a single translation robs the author of rhetorical force and the listener of the chance to consider all the various functions of the Holy Spirit. The Holy Spirit is specifically said to do the following: teach, remind (14:26), abide (14:16), and testify about Jesus (15:26). Like Jesus, the Holy Spirit deals in truth. True to his word, the Word breathes (*emphysaō*) the Holy Spirit upon his disciples (20:22), making them one with God and Jesus.

Through the language of abiding (*menō*), love, being "in" (14:17, 20), and, later in the Discourse, "one-ness" (17:21–23), John insists that the intimate relationship between him, God, and the Spirit also includes believers.

As I've noted repeatedly, Jesus refers quite often to coming and going; he does so again in verse 18. He comes in different ways, of course: through the Holy Spirit, through the peace he gives, and so forth. But pause now to really absorb verse 18, where Jesus promises, "I will not leave y'all orphaned; I am coming to you." Two things about this statement stop me up short. First, Jesus keeps all of his promises: We. Are. Never. Alone. It's rare for me to say that something is not debatable. This is not debatable. It's bedrock truth.

Second, the orphan language hits me in so many different ways, from the personal to the global level. On the personal level, I am half adopted; I've never met my biological father. I have no idea if he's dead or alive. I do, however, know my real father, the one who has faithfully parented me since I was four years old and has always been part of what *home* means to me. As a career Navy family, we've had lots of houses in my lifetime. So my notions of family and home are not literal. I'm unimpressed by family defined by biology or home defined by buildings. But that's me.

On the global level, as I write, unprecedented numbers of people have been displaced from the place they called home and are refugees or migrants for a number of painful reasons. Many are, quite literally, orphaned and homeless. What does Jesus' promise look like here on the ground in these places? Where do we fit into this global reality?

The believer is a participant, not a bystander in the relationship he describes. Verse 23 is the pinnacle of the passage: "Jesus answered him, 'Those who love me will keep my word, and my Father will love them, and we will come to them and make our home with them.'" If God, Jesus, and the Spirit abide *en* (the Greek word means both "in" and "among") us (14:7), have made their home with us (recall 1:14), how can we imagine any distance between us and God? This, in turn, affects our eschatology (our view of the end, the goal to which all things are headed, now or later). Everything that matters—ultimate intimacy with God and Christ—is available *now*. What might one hope for beyond that? God is not currently holding out on us in any way. Abundant life, embodied life, eternal life, precious life, is here for the living, from this very moment into eternity.

It's worth noting that love is tied to John's emphasis on the present, rather than on just a delayed future time of history's fulfillment. Jesus gives one commandment: to love. Therefore, judgment and eternal life begin now. For John, at the end of each day and during each moment of each day, there's only one question to ask yourself: "In what ways did I love or did I not love today?" As you reflect upon that, judgment happens. Where you did not love, therein lies judgment. But for John judgment is merely diagnostic, not retributive. Jesus constantly asks the characters questions that help them understand their lives and motives more clearly. To the sick man in 5:6: "Do you wish to be made well?"; to Martha in 11:26: "Do you believe this?" He asks questions, not because he doesn't know the answers (2:24–25 assures us that Jesus already knows everything); rather, he asks so that we may know and therefore move forward with clear vision into the truth, light, glory, love, and abundant life for which God has created us. It's all of a piece, now and forever.

Jesus closes the chapter with a blessing of peace, using words similar to the opening. He consoles them, he acknowledges the dark days ahead, he indicates that he is almost done talking, and he says, "Rise, let us be going." But then he proceeds to talk for three more chapters! This puzzling fact is tied to this Gospel's layered history of composition. That need not detain us here. Instead, let's take a look at what he has to say next in chapter 15. Unlike Mark's Jesus, John's Jesus is quite a Wordy person!

Questions for Reflection

I have always been drawn to John's repeated language of Christian community as our home and our family. Therefore, I find myself collecting poems and songs that have home as a central metaphor. I invite you to choose one of the following:

- Sit with John 14. Quickly glance through the whole Gospel of John, looking at the language of family and home.
- Sit with one of these:
  - "Wild Geese" by Mary Oliver. You can hear her read it at http://www.onbeing.org/blog/mary-oliver-reads-wild-geese/5966.
  - "HOME," by Somali poet Warsan Shire, http://seekershub.org/blog/2015/09/home-warsan-shire/.
  - "Finally Home" by Justin Froese, https://justinfroese.bandcamp.com/track/finally-here-2.

Chapter 10

Lively, Life-Giving Friendship

John 15

Among other wonders of our lives, we are alive
with one another, we walk here
in the light of this unlikely world
that isn't ours for long.
May we spend generously
the time we are given.
May we enact our responsibilities
as thoroughly as we enjoy
our pleasures. May we see with clarity,
may we seek a vision
that serves all beings, may we honor
the mystery surpassing our sight,
and may we hold in our hands
the gift of good work
and bear it forth whole, as we
were borne forth by a power we praise
to this one Earth, this homeland of all we love.

John Daniel, "Prayer among Friends"[1]

I recently had cause to consider and admire the power of deep, authentic friendship. When our son Caleb was five months old, we moved to Dallas. As Providence would have it, we were dropped down right next to the Kramers, who also had a five-month-old son. His name? Joshua. I kid you not. (If you don't follow me here, refer

1. John Daniel, "A Prayer among Friends," in *Of Earth: New and Selected Poems* (Sandpoint, ID: Lost Horse Press, 2012). Reprinted with permission. See http://writersalmanac.publicradio.org/index.php?date=2012/10/19.

to Num. 13–14 and, of course, the book of Joshua.) Fifteen years later, they are still best friends (and Josh's mom, Kim, is still Caleb's other mother), even though when they were nine we moved three-quarters of a mile to a new house (against Caleb's heart-wrenching protests, wherein, among other things, he begged us to take all of his money in his bank account and buy the house back from the buyers), and even though they chose to go to different high schools. When they were fifteen, I got to take them on a road trip to Austin for the RTX event, an Internet gaming extravaganza. Just the three of us. I laughed much (understand that I have no brothers). And I learned a lot about Internet gaming; about being a fifteen-year-old male; and about the gift of a truly solid, unconditional, faithful friendship between two people who are somewhat similar but also very different from each other.

Friendship is a form of covenant. Covenant, of course, is a relational word, a communal word. God makes a covenant with God's people, collectively speaking. If we want to strengthen our covenant with God, we have to strengthen our relationships with one another. There's just no getting around it. Today, many of us imagine our relationship with God in very individualistic ways. It's me, Jesus, and my Bible. We don't necessarily assume that our fate depends upon a community. But no biblical person in either the Old Testament or the New Testament would have envisioned a relationship with God as anything separate from the community's relationship with God.

We are all connected, whether we like it or not. What we do or don't do does, in fact, affect the community, near and far. "Live together, die alone," as the saying goes. We are damned together or saved together. This is why Jesus harps so much on the organic language of vines and branches and, finally, on the language of friendship and love. If we are not a community marked by friendship and love, then we should close up shop. If we are not a community with friendship and love as our key goals and markers, then we may be many things, some even useful and worthwhile, but we are not a *Christian* community. But don't take my word for it. Let's look at John 15, another part of the Farewell Discourse Jesus delivers to his disciples.

The chapter begins with this "I am" statement, the last one in the Gospel: "I am the true vine, and my Father is the vinegrower." Already we see dependence and mutuality and cooperation that bears fruit; here it's between Jesus and God. The whole garden belongs to God; and why wouldn't it? Remember John 1:3: "All things came into being through him, and without him not one thing came into being." Chapter 20 finds resurrected Jesus walking in a garden where Mary Magdalene mistakes him not for *a* gardener but for *the* Gardener. John draws heavily on Old Testament imagery in which Israel is portrayed as God's vineyard (Isa. 5:1–7). The Old Testament is very concerned about Israel's bearing fruit by responding faithfully to God's word (see Ps. 1:3). In 15:5 Jesus expands the image to include the role of the disciples—and therefore, us. Hear this important statement and take it personally. Jesus says, "I am the vine, you are the branches. Those who abide in me and I in them bear much fruit, because apart from me you can do nothing."

There you have it. Jesus is the vine; we are the branches. We abide in him, and he abides in us. The word translated "abide" here, *menō*, is a favorite word of John's. Sixteen of the twenty-one chapters have it; it occurs over forty times. Additionally, the noun form occurs at 14:2: "In my Father's house there are many dwelling places (*monai*)." In some sense it refers back to 1:14 and dwelling, as well as to all of the house/home language flagged throughout. It is a deeply relational word and can be translated as "abide," "remain," or "stay." "And the slave does not remain in the house forever; the son does remain forever" (8:35). Believers and Jesus abide in one another: "Those who eat my flesh and drink my blood abide in me, and I in them" (6:56). Abiding is important.

Jesus energizes us to bear fruit. But what does it mean for us to bear fruit? It means we are to love. Yes, to *love*.

> As the Father has *loved* me, so I have *loved* you; abide in my *love*. If you keep my commandments, you will abide in my *love*, just as I have kept my Father's commandments and abide in his *love*. . . . This is my commandment, that you *love* one another as I have *loved* you. No one has greater *love* than this, to lay down one's life for one's friends. You are my friends if you do what I command you. . . . I am giving you these commands so that you may *love* one another. (vv. 9–10, 12–14, 17)

This final "I am" statement is consumed with love. We are not merely servants of Jesus; we are his friends. The Greek word for "friend," *philos*, comes from one of the verbs for love (*phileō*). Another word often used for "love" in this Gospel comes from *agapē*. The "I am" statements in John show us that God in Christ is intent not only on *life* but also on *love*. They go hand in hand. Notice that Jesus does not ask us to do anything that he himself has not already done, even to the point of laying down one's life for one's friends.

We are branches. If we stay connected to the true vine, Jesus, which is nurtured by God, the vinegrower, we will bear the fruits of love. If we don't, we won't. We will hate, just as the world hates (15:9). The choice is ours: Will we be counted among the lovers or the haters? Where are you on the spectrum at present?

Radical, Authentic Friendship

This is about Jesus loving his disciples and his disciples loving one another. In other words, this is about how to be and do Christian community. It's about radical friendship. How is your church doing this well? How could it do better? What is your own role in this?

Obstacles

What are the obstacles to radical, authentic friendships, in your experience? Here are a few I've encountered; you can add others.

Competition. Sometimes followers of Jesus compete when they should cooperate. While John contains neither the story of the disciples fighting over who is best (Matt. 18:1–5; Mark 9:33–37; Luke 9:46–48) nor the competition of who will get to sit on Jesus' right and left (Matt. 20:20–28; Mark 10:35–45), it has other, unique stories about competition between disciples. For instance, in chapter 20, Peter and the Beloved Disciple compete to be the second one to the tomb (Mary Magdalene is the first). In chapter 21, Peter competes with the Beloved Disciple, worrying that the Beloved Disciple is getting a better deal than he is, to which Jesus responds, "Follow me."

Pride. Pride can assure us that we don't need anyone else.

Trust issues. Trust can be a difficult one. If you've lived long enough, you have betrayed someone else's trust, and you have been hurt by failed trust. Remember Judas? Brené Brown has certainly helped us all with her work on the importance of daring to be vulnerable. In fact, her research has shown that being vulnerable is essential to living what she calls a "wholehearted" life. Her book *Daring Greatly* is a helpful resource in this regard (she also has a TED talk on it). What makes it more difficult for some of us is that our deepest hurts around trust have come from church, the one place we thought we could be most vulnerable. But healing can happen, and we must forge ahead in creating spaces of trust and vulnerability in Christian community, no matter what the past has held.

Shame or guilt. Some of us have failed in a way that makes us ashamed and wanting to hide or run away from our earlier dreams or sense of calling or giftedness. Imagine how Peter felt on that boat with his community, the other disciples. It took an additional visit with Jesus to regain himself and his purpose.

Fear. There are probably as many fears as there are people. Fears of all sorts separate us and supply the ego with horrendous lies about "the other." If we were honest, we could build an impressive list of why it's a bad (or at least naive) idea to reach out in friendship, especially across perceived barriers. Remember the disciples' reaction when Jesus befriended the Samaritan woman?

A theology of scarcity vs. a theology of abundance. Sometimes we believe that more for someone else means less for me. Or that gifts like love and friendship are a precious commodity that must be doled out in a very measured way lest someone gets something they don't deserve (like Judas at the meal in chap. 13), or won't use correctly, or won't receive with enough gratitude. There is enough. There is more than enough. How might we relax into that certain knowledge?

Remedies

If we have listed some of the obstacles in attempting radical, authentic friendship, might we imagine some possible ways forward?

Rituals. Churches know the power of rituals. What might a covenant ritual look like for those looking to live in intentional Christian community with one another? What might a "recovery from betrayal" ritual look like? I recently completed a "congregational health" questionnaire for my church. It had a lot of questions on it that you'd expect. But this one caught me off guard: "Do members forgive one another?" What a question! I wasn't really sure how to answer it, upon what basis to make the judgment call. I'm still pondering that. All churches, all relationships that matter, are destined to have painful conflict. Do we have rituals that allow us to be honest about naming those and repairing the relationship? I was sitting with a group of fellow members as a team of folks charged with helping our church move into her future story. We were meeting in a room normally used for Sunday School. On the wall was a poster that said this: "The need to let suffering speak is a condition of all truth." I was struck by how many of us noticed and commented on the poster, wondering if it was placed there by the leader as part of our meeting. Turns out, the class that meets in there (and put the poster up) was studying the book of Job.

I imagine not only rituals for entering covenantal relationships of various kinds and rituals of healing from betrayal, but also rituals for acknowledging the end of a covenantal relationship, such as divorce or departing from one worshiping community to join another. Can you think of others?

Structured relationships. What are some structures that could train us in the ways of this radical, authentic friendship?

> *Mentors/mentees*. Here I have in mind a structured (however loosely) relationship between a person who has more experience in life, a particular job, or a particular area of spiritual giftedness and a person who is intentionally seeking development in such an area.
>
> *Accountability partners*. For some readers, this may sound draconian and oppressive. For others, you have enjoyed the structure and regularity of touching base with someone else as you aim to conform your life more closely to that of Jesus. It's a thing worth considering.
>
> *Coaches*
>
> *Deep, spiritual friendships*

Small groups. The vine and the branches, bearing fruits of love, always in community. "I give you a new commandment, that you love one another. Just as I have loved you, you also should love one another. By this everyone will know that you are my disciples, if you have love for one another" (13:34–35). It's crucial to practice loving one another in concrete ways, which is best done in small groups. It's easy to love humanity in general, but it can be a little more challenging to love particular people in our community week in and week out.

> "I'm no longer calling you servants because servants don't understand what their master is thinking and planning. No, I've named you friends because I've let you in on everything I've heard from the Father.
>
> "You didn't choose me, remember; I chose you, and put you in the world to bear fruit, fruit that won't spoil. As fruit bearers, whatever you ask the Father in relation to me, he gives you.
>
> "But remember the root command: Love one another." (15:15–17, *The Message*)

Do you presently enjoy such friendship? Do you presently offer such friendship?

Questions for Reflection

1. In this passage, Jesus is specifically talking to his own followers about friendship within their own community. Do you think your friendship with other Christians is similar to or different from your friendship with those who are not Christian? Should there be any differences?
2. Take some time now to experience this performance by one of my favorite spoken word poets, Allyson Wermelskirchen (who guest-visits my classes from time to time). You'll be glad you did! Here are the words to it (don't skip her embodied performance, though).[2]

I Am the Vine

Jesus came from the father
from the gardener who plants us

2. See more from Allyson Wermelskirchen at http://vimeo.com/91338557 and http://www.allysonwerm.com.

he said, I am the vine
and you are the branches
If you remain in me and I remain in you
together there can be much fruit
but apart from me
there can be none

I am the vine that feeds you
when you need to be nourished
I am the only way you will flourish
the veins in my vine course with courage
stream with strength
and swell with love
extended to you
so that you can do what
the gardener intended
so that when He tends us
He will be pleased by what you yield.

I am the stem that won't let you wilt
that will keep you standing though this life may tilt
though the world has the power to jilt
I am the rod that replants and rebuilds
restores and redeems
I have the power to plants seeds
for the Gardener to harvest
The same Gardener who plants light
and plucks out darkness
the same Gardener-God who made us in his likeness
who made us to bear fruit
and without whom we're destitute
but with whom we are resolutely
purposed with the potential to produce

He said I am the vine, I carry the roots
I'm asking you not to cut me loose
or use me as noose
for I am the vine which gives life

I am the vine which can revive
from which you were derived
The vine by which you thrive
I am your key to survival,
and your hope for new life
the fullest way to come alive
the truest way to come alive
the *only* way to come alive
I am the vine and you are the branches
I am the giver of second chances
I am the vine
I am the soil
I am the sunshine
I am the rain
I am the remedy
I am the truth,
the hope,
the love,
I am the vine
and

I am the life

Chapter 11

All Is Lost, All Is Gained

John 16

When I consider the bitter sweetness of this chapter of the Farewell Discourse, where all is lost but all is gained, a number of images and experiences come to mind. Have you ever sent a child off into the world? On the one hand, you know and are committed to the fact that it's best for your child to leave home and fulfill her or his destiny, with all of the beauty and danger that surely attends such a quest. On the other hand, you just want to cling tightly, rewatch all of their favorite movies from childhood, and snuggle them to sleep.

The week before my daughter left for college, we were watching *Brother Bear*, one of our favorite movies. It's full of wisdom about the joys and suffering that life holds; it's also visually beautiful and inspiring. As we watched Koda and Kenai meet and listened that time around to the young bear Koda sing "On My Way," it struck me as a perfect "leaving home" song. It also strikes me as a somewhat useful way to tap into the emotion and content of chapter 16. I encourage you to pause reading for just a few moments to look up the lyrics and listen to the song on the Internet. No, really—go listen to it! It begins like this:

> Tell everybody I'm on my way
> New friends and new places to see

When I mentioned how this song applies to leaving home, my daughter said, "I didn't think about it like that." I said, "It's *all* I think about lately!" You see things differently, depending on your perspective. Where one person anticipates new, greater possibilities, the other may feel a sense of grief or loss.

Jesus is always coming and going in John; he stays on the move. He descends from and ascends to God; he traverses territories of land and the human soul. In fact, he redefines "home" itself. Jesus does not grieve here—quite the opposite. While he acknowledges their grief, he sees what they cannot yet see through the tears that cloud their eyes: joy awaits them. The song says nothing will stop Koda from setting out; the same goes for Jesus.

Like a mother in labor (or moving her child into a dorm), the disciples' pain is real. But that's only part of the story; they will also receive the gift of the Holy Spirit. In fact, Jesus says that their receiving the Spirit *depends upon* his going away (16:7).

And they will see Jesus again, and again, and again: "A little while, and you will no longer see me, and again a little while, and you will see me" (16:16). In *Brother Bear*, we watch Koda return to his home community after his adventure and hear:

> 'Cause there's nothing like seeing
> Each other again

I don't know that the disciples want to rewatch old movies or snuggle Jesus to sleep, but I do know that they want to cling to Jesus' physical presence (as does Mary in chap. 20).

Grief can cause disconnect and confusion. At the opening of the chapter, Jesus predicts a difficult road ahead for his followers, maybe even death. They say nothing, and Jesus notes that aloud: "But now I am going to him who sent me; yet none of you asks me, 'Where are you going?'" (16:5). This is a little puzzling, since the issue of where Jesus is going has come up repeatedly in the Gospel. "The Jews" and Pharisees are always confused about it (7:11, 32; 8:14). Peter tries in chapter 13:

> "Little children, I am with you only a little longer. You will look for me; and as I said to the Jews so now I say to you, 'Where I am going, you cannot come.' . . .
>
> Simon Peter said to him, "Lord, where are you going?" Jesus answered, "Where I am going, you cannot follow me now; but you will follow afterward." (13:33–36)

In the next chapter, Thomas takes a stab at it:

> "If it were not so, would I have told you that I go to prepare a place for you? And if I go and prepare a place for you, I will come again and will take you to myself, so that where I am, there you may be also. And you know the way to the place where I am going." Thomas said to him, "Lord, we do not know where you are going. How can we know the way?" Jesus said to him, "I am the way, and the truth, and the life. No one comes to the Father except through me." (14:2–6)

This time around, they don't ask. Why do you think that is the case? "But because I have said these things to you, sorrow has filled your hearts" (16:6). They sit in what I imagine to be stunned silence. What are they feeling? What are they thinking? Can they imagine the joy on the other side of their pain?

So Jesus keeps talking. He provokes them by, once again, saying that he's leaving but that they will see him again (v. 17). They bite this time. They come out of silence but not out of their grief stupor. I love the exchange that happens next. They are just kind of "done" with Jesus at this point. They look at each other (roll their eyes? squinch up their eyes, raise their shoulders up to their ears and hold their arms out, bent at the elbows, with their palms up to signify: "What is this guy talking about?"). Finally, they say frankly, "We don't know what he's talking about" (v. 18; my trans.). He intervenes and calls them out on their pooled ignorance and failure to question the source. But in the past when they've asked, they've met with other cryptic statements, from their point of view.

Remember that you, the reader, are the audience for the writer, and the author is using the disciples as literary characters to teach you something. You, the reader, have been given all kinds of information that the disciples as literary characters are not privy to. You also already know how the story turns out; they don't. You already know that Jesus will be raised, appear multiple times, ascend to God, send the Spirit, and guide the church for two thousand years. They don't. They can't, until the events unfold in their proper order. Everything that is said in the Gospel is for your benefit as the reader/hearer.

As soon as Jesus uses an analogy from their regular lives, they begin to understand. These men imagine themselves as birthing mothers. They latch onto the image of moving from pain to joy. Who doesn't want to leave pain and rush to joy as quickly as possible? The disciples get whiplash as they jerk their heads from the one extreme of sorrow to the other extreme of joy and answered prayer. They are quickly on board again, loving all of this upbeat talk and promises, confessing their devotion (vv. 29–30). Remember that this same pattern happens with Peter at the end of chapter 13. And what happens there happens again here. Jesus gives them a reality check about how discipleship in the real world works. They will all falter, not just Peter: "The hour is coming, indeed it has come, when y'all will be scattered, each one to his home, and y'all will leave me alone" (16:32, my trans.). There is no easy fix, and you can't get to solid joy by doing an end run around the evil, hatred, and death in the world that touches us all. The only way to Easter is through the cross.

When we are in our right minds, we know this. Our artists know this. Think of the epic stories you know from antiquity to the present that have most profoundly shaped you and stuck with you; they know this. I'm tempted to say, "Life isn't a fairy tale," but some versions of the fairy tales face the darkness head-on and don't offer the easy, saccharine ending. Have you seen the play (now also a movie) *Into the Woods*? I find it brilliant. (I'm partial to the version with Bernadette Peters in it.) As one friend, Nathan Russell, wrote about it on Facebook: "There's something about going out into the world—the wood—and discovering both who and what we are. Terrifying and wondrous all at the same time." What else is the cross, the life of discipleship, if not "terrifying and wondrous all at the same time"?

Tobias Wolff hits the nail on the head in his foreword to a collection of short stories (I think it applies to Scripture as well):

> As it happens, many of the stories in this book confront difficult material: violence, sickness, alcoholism, sexual exploitation, marital breakup. Well, so do we. I have never been able to understand the complaint that a story is "depressing" because of its subject matter. What depresses me are stories that don't seem to know these things go on, or hide them in resolute chipperness; "witty" stories, in which every problem is an occasion for a joke, "upbeat" stories that flog you with transcendence. Please. We're grown-ups now, we get to stay in the kitchen when the other grown-ups talk. . . . Far from being depressed, my own reaction

> to stories like these is exhilaration, both at the honesty and the art. The art gives shape to what the honesty discovers, allows us to face what in truth we were already afraid of anyway. It lets us know we're not alone.[1]

Not alone. Jesus reveals to the disciples that they will all leave him alone. But that is not the last word of his story. Or theirs. Or ours. "Yet I am not alone because the Father is with me. I have said this to you, so that in me you may have peace. In the world you face persecution. But take courage; I have conquered the world!" (vv. 32–33).

I love the way that chapter 16 (and our whole Christian tradition, for that matter) insists that, far from being opposites, lament and joy belong together. The same is true for truth and hope. Those who grieve in hope know this in their heart of hearts. It is not "unchristian" to lament; lamenting doesn't keep us from joy—it is part of the journey back to joy. And the harsh truth of loss and death does not preclude hope. It's our ability to speak our (painful) truth that makes way for the hope. We can hope boldly because, as Jesus teaches the disciples here, the final word with God is never ultimate separation but eternal connection, however unimaginable it might seem to us at the moment.

You might argue that the scientists are our best mystics these days. In the past, Christians have been quite comfortable with the notion that there is more to reality than meets the eye; that the communion of saints exists; that visions and dreams and experiences of those who have passed away are real. When I'm not teaching John, I'm often teaching on my other favorite subject—"Evil, Suffering, Death, and Afterlife." I always find myself (tenderly) amused when I lead multiday seminars on this and during the breaks or at the end of the day, people approach me to share a profound experience they've had with someone who has died or some other experience of having a revelation or insight at a particular time that turns out to coincide with something happening to someone in their life at the exact same time. They speak in hushed tones and ask me if they are crazy. They are normal, everyday people who are running kids to baseball practice,

1. Tobias Wolff, *The Vintage Book of American Short Stories* (New York: Vintage Contemporaries, 1994), xv.

reading bestsellers, hoping for a more peaceful world, and so on. I smile in appreciation for their sharing such meaningful events with me and assure them (and you) that such experiences appear in our tradition from Genesis to Revelation, from the first century to the twenty-first. They may not be common, but they are not unique.

Have you ever had such an experience? Or, in your grief, have you longed to connect across time and space with your loved one and met with disappointment? Do you expect, finally, to be "surprised by joy"?

> *Prayer: Jesus, help us to face the difficulties of life with honesty about ourselves, the people in our lives, and the conditions of the world. Give us courage to set out into the wood/world anyway. Give us a sense of peace based on the knowledge that we are never alone. Ever. Amen.*

Questions for Reflection

1. I once saw a necklace that says, "I choose joy." Is joy really a choice? If so, how hard is it to choose? Do you choose it?
2. Reflect on a time when your grief eclipsed (or at least threatened) your joy. Did grief finally give way to joy? Is that how it works? Did you find a way to put the two in conversation with one another? What did that conversation sound like? Does that conversation ever end or just change?
3. Do you know someone who has remained overwhelmed by grief? What does the "good news" look like in such a situation?
4. Jesus is clearly comfortable with the notion of moving between heaven and earth, between repeatedly coming and going, between different states of being (preexistence, earthly existence, eternal existence). Are you? Celtic Christians speak of "thin spaces."
5. Our contemporary physicists and cosmologists and philosophers continue to ponder the nature of reality itself. It appears we have been thinking (and living?) too small. How many dimensions are there? (Somewhere between three and twenty-six.) What about parallel universes? What is the smallest unit of being (atoms are so "yesterday"; we are now on [super] string theory)? Do you find the mysterious and the mystical intriguing, inspiring, or irrelevant?

Chapter 12

"That They May Be One," or Unity, Jesus-Style

John 17

We now finally come to the true end of the Farewell Discourse. And what does Jesus focus on? Oneness. Why is it important to him? What does he mean by it? What are the promises and pitfalls of trying to make his dream a reality here and now?

In some ways, there's a surge in interest in oneness. From Richard Rohr's work with the unified field (see, e.g., *Falling Upward*) to the scientists working on the "theory of everything," our imaginations are being stoked toward deeper thought and maturity.

Recently I was privileged to see and hear His Holiness the 14th Dalai Lama; we even got to sing "Happy Birthday" to him for his eightieth birthday (along with thousands of other folks). He spoke of compassion and cooperation and the power of a unified vision. I was inspired and shared the experience for the next couple of days. I was a bit taken aback by more than one negative reaction from people who couldn't imagine how the Dalai Lama, a Buddhist, could have anything to teach me, a Christian. They made two moves that seem to be so typical and are part and parcel of the human condition. First, they immediately jumped to differences: this is *different from* that. Second, they moved to hierarchy: this is *better than* that. Such moves lead us away from compassion, cooperation, and the power of a unified vision.

The Farewell Discourse concludes with Jesus' farewell prayer, where Jesus prays to God in the presence of and on behalf of his followers. Three themes are prominent, and none is new in John: unity, glorification, and knowledge.

"One" is used 345 times in the NT. It appears 32 times in John, from start to finish literally: 1:3, 40; 3:27; 6:8, 22, 70–71; 7:21, 50; 8:9, 41; 9:25; 10:16, 30; 11:49–50, 52; 12:2, 4; 13:21, 23; 17:11, 21–23; 18:14, 22, 26, 39; 19:34; 20:1, 7, 12, 19, 24; 21:25.

The prayer is divided into three parts. In verses 1–8, Jesus prays for his own glorification. Jesus' own unity with God is highlighted here. In verses 9–19, Jesus prays for his disciples. Here is the logic: Jesus acted in unity with God and did his job/work so that the first disciples benefited from it. Now those disciples are to act in unity with Jesus so that future disciples will benefit. In fact, those future disciples (i.e., we) are in view in verses 20–26. So now we are to act in unity with the disciples so that the whole world benefits. Always, the life of the world is in view. Throughout the Gospel, Jesus works for integration/unity at all levels: the self (Peter), the community (Farewell Discourse), the world, the cosmos.

The Call to Unity: Risking Our Lives with and for Each Other

When Jesus prays here, it's not magic and it's not just a wish. Rather, he wills what he is praying. His will is in line with God's, so it is done. Now we just have to act as if it's true.

Why should we? First, we thrive as individuals and communities when we are living the lives we were created to live, spiritual lives that are, by design, embodied and communal. We have big words for it, like "incarnational" and "ecclesiological," but it means we are very much a part of God's created order, and the job is not to distance ourselves from the messiness of it all, but to jump in, full force. When you do, we'll wash your feet with a basin and a towel (or maybe just a baby wipe, if that's what's handy). Second, we please God by fulfilling the charge to do greater works than Jesus himself did. Not just "think greater thoughts," mind you, but "do greater works." See the Prologue and John 3:16: God created it, redeems it, and sustains it. Shouldn't we be in the same business?

What are the obstacles? Let's get this conversation out of the way quickly. I know there are as many reasons to avoid unity as there are people. We have lots of reasons: competition, a theology of scarcity instead of abundance (recall Mary and Judas), too busy, don't want the same things, don't want to be in each other's business, don't like conflict. The bottom line? It's complicated, and it may cost us something. Recall the Ubuntu saying "I am because we are." If we have a hundred reasons why we can't do it, the Bible has a hundred examples of how we can.

Unity

The Farewell Discourse pulls the disciples inside: we see footwashing, reclining with one another, eating together, sharing sorrow. For unity to work, we must do life together—the most basic, dirty, scary, intimate parts of it. We have to be vulnerable and honest. That means we are going to get our toes stepped on, and we are going to do some embarrassing things. We are going to have to learn how to forgive and be forgiven. Before the disciples can be transformative agents in their world, they must *first* become unified. For some this is easy. They welcome change and don't know why anyone would have a problem with it. Others feel fear or grief and need more time to adjust. Others are resigned, like Thomas! At 14:31 Jesus says, "Rise, let us be going." Those who are ready to move would jump right up. But Jesus talks for three more chapters; he gives them details, time, and prayer. The prayer teaches us that unity is a gift from God, and it is possible—if we depend on Jesus, who wills this very thing for us.

Their unity is not just for their own benefit, however. Yes, he has taken them aside to form them and teach them how to do unity, how to do life together; but he has never intended for them (or us) to stay in their little sanctuary. He's only been preparing them to go and do life with the world, the way he does. He crosses every boundary known to his time. Sometimes he seeks out the encounters instead of waiting for people to come to him (e.g., the Samaritan woman in chap. 4; the man at Bethesda in chap. 5; the man who is blind in chap. 9); missional churches today are doing creative work in this area. Sometimes he just engages as he goes, but he's done the prep work to be fruitful in the encounter.

What dualisms still inhibit us? Can you name some you've noticed in the past week? Here are a few: sacred/profane; body/soul; white/black; Christian/not-Christian; disabled/nondisabled; religion/politics; prayer/action; charity/justice; faith/works. Perhaps the most trenchant one of all is us/them. What would it take for us to question the either/or approach and embrace the both/and, to abandon false, even destructive, dualisms that keep us acting more like Judas and less like Mary? We are called to be a missional church, and we can't do that unless we are involved in the most touchy, most vulnerable, most meaningful, most saving work that stands before us. If we are just a salon of sorts, a glorified book club, a group that gathers to bat around interesting (even controversial) ideas, a historical society whose chief aim is to protect our glorious heritage, then let's, for starters, at least have the decency to stop calling ourselves a church, for Christ's sake—and for sure, let's stop calling ourselves a *Christian* church.

A cord of three strands is not easily broken, Ecclesiastes 4:12 insists; so how much more so a cord of four strands: believers are unified with God, Christ, the Spirit, and one another. Therefore, we are strong and equipped to do greater works than Jesus. There's no reason we can't demonstrate and reveal God's love for everything in God's cosmos just as effectively as Jesus did. This is an empowering word, to be sure; it's also a challenging word, because we cannot pretend to be waiting for something God has yet to provide before we get on with the work at hand. We can't wring our hands and say, "If only . . ." To be sure, the road will be rough enough that Jesus feels the need to offer prayers for our protection as we go; we know then that we are in good hands. We have all we need to testify to God's love in ways that will bring abundant life, embodied life, eternal life, precious life to all of creation.

Knowledge

How does John define eternal life? It's being in relationship with God and Christ, what John calls "knowing" them, and it's available in its entirety now. Recall that Jesus knew everything about the Samaritan woman. Of course he did, since we already learned in 2:25 that he knew what was in everyone and had no need for anyone to tell him anything. This is the deepest kind of knowing, as in Psalm 139. When all is said and done, what deeper desire exists than to know and be truly known, to understand and be truly understood, to love and be truly loved? According to John, that's the meaning of life.

This Gospel specializes in "knowing" language (*ginōskō, oida*) and "loving" language (*agapaō, phileō*), because they go together. This may seem counterintuitive to us. We may assume the opposite, in fact. We take great pains to hide true knowledge of ourselves, since we assume that the more someone knows the real me, the less love they will have for me. As knowledge goes up, love goes down; if we want love to remain high, then we'd better work hard to pass ourselves off as "lovable."

John takes issue with such moves. Can you really deeply love that which you do not know? Knowing depends upon authentic relationship and regular encounter with the beloved. Is it any wonder that four great examples of discipleship in John are the Samaritan woman in chapter 4, the blind man in chapter 9, Mary in chapter 12, and Thomas, of all people, in chapter 19? What do they have in common? They each participate in ongoing relationship and encounter with Jesus. Both the Samaritan woman and the man born blind have lengthy, increasingly deep dialogue with Jesus; as they do, they understand him more and more, to the point where they know him and understand that he is the source of their lives and loves them like no other. This leads them to worship him and testify to others about him.

Mary is described as one whom Jesus loves (11:5), and John makes it clear that she, her brother Lazarus, and sister Martha regularly spend time with Jesus. Thomas may be a less obvious hero, but he's a hero nonetheless in this Gospel. He sticks with Jesus even though he discerns that trouble is in store (11:16); he asks questions when he doesn't understand (14:5); he's not gullible or prone to flights of fancy, but he's willing to believe when confronted with raw glory (chap. 20). On the basis of all of this, Thomas comes to know Jesus fully, such that he declares him to be "my Lord and my God" (20:28).

Glorification

Whatever the relationship between Jesus and God entails, glorification is a substantial part of it. In 7:39 we learn that believers have *not yet* received the Spirit because Jesus has not yet been glorified. The bestowal of the Spirit in John is entirely dependent upon Jesus' death and resurrection. In John, the death and resurrection are not a denigration of any sort; rather, they are described in terms of coronation, exaltation, and glorification. What was yet to be in 7:39 is now realized as Jesus says, "Father, the hour has come" (17:1). The glory buildup starts in chapter 12 with the end of Jesus' public ministry and his turn to his closest companions. The process starts with Mary anointing Jesus' feet for his burial and Jesus' indication that "the hour has come for the Son of Man to be glorified" (12:23). It's an interesting feature of John that the passion, resurrection, and ascension are all considered as one moment rather than individual, linear, discrete events. We call chapters 1–12 the Book of Signs and chapters 13–21 the Book of Glory. "Glory" (*doxa*) and "glorify" (*doxazō*) appear forty-two times in John, most of them in chapters 13–21. More than one-third of all NT occurrences of the verb "glorify" occur in John.

While most occurrences appear in the latter part of the Gospel, from the beginning the reader is made to understand that seeing Jesus in the flesh means seeing the glory of God: "And the Word became flesh and lived among us, and we have seen his glory, the glory as of a father's only son, full of grace and truth" (1:14). The rest of the Gospel details the evidence of that glory and, more surprisingly, our own participation in it. God's glory in John is like being at the very heart of a fireworks display rather than watching it on TV. You see the light, feel the thunder, find yourself breathless, caught up in the majesty and power and wonder and extraordinary transcendence of it all. You look around and find that others have come seeking something of this wonder too; so for a moment you're connected with other pilgrims who have braved the journey rather than settling for a secondhand account of the thing.

John's notion of God's glory is informed by the Old Testament, which speaks much about the "glory of the Lord." Exodus looms large in the author's imagination. Consider Exodus 40:35: "Moses was not able to enter the tent of meeting because the cloud settled upon it, and the glory of the Lord filled the tabernacle." The "glory of the Lord" is God's presence. The word for tabernacle here in the Greek version (LXX) of Exodus (*skēnē*) is the same word that appears in John 1:14, which tells us that the Word became flesh and "tabernacled" among us. Jesus becomes the locus of God's presence.

Then Jesus draws us fully into that presence. With every word, the author of John pushes to intimacy. The incarnation, glory, love, father, mother, son, one, knowing—every last word declares that God created this world, with the help of Jesus, for the single purpose of unity with all of creation. Jesus models and completes that unity. Jesus glorifies God by completing the works God sent him to do.

The baton gets passed in the same way, of course, from Jesus to believers, who will do greater works than Jesus. Now believers glorify God when they reveal God's loving presence to the world God created and will love to the end (3:16), even as that world shows resistance, even hatred. No matter; the job is done; Jesus has conquered the world (16:33). John's tenses are confusing to us, because he often speaks as if something that is in the process of happening, or has not yet happened, has already happened. But from God's perspective, these things are so certain that they can be spoken of as already complete. This is why believers go forth in confidence, with undying hope, despite the way things appear.

The author has not given up on the world. Jesus prays for the world later in chapter 17. If he had given up on the world, Jesus would not have equipped the disciples with power equal to his own to do their part in unifying the world to God. Believers do indeed belong to Jesus, have been given to him; but everything belongs to God and will ultimately be drawn to God through Christ's work (12:32).

> ***Prayer:*** *Rise, let us be going (14:31). God, may your blessings be upon us as we go out in unity to be agents of deep and unifying change. Amen.*

Chapter 13

Crowning the King of Israel: The Passion

John 18–19

*I*f there ever was proof that the author expects you to read all the way through in order, it's in the arrest, trial, crucifixion, and resurrection. All things preceding come to full fruition now, and the attentive reader will recall the connections. I'll help.

Act 1: The Betrayal and Arrest

Scene 1: Arrest in a Garden

I recommend that as we go, you imagine the story on film. It opens in a garden (in fact, many important stories in the Bible are set in a garden). How did Judas know where to find Jesus? Because Jesus regularly met there with his followers. A space that was normally reserved for coming together to worship and learn more about God's kingdom is directly invaded by the kingdoms of this world, by evil.

I can't help but think here of Oscar Romero, archbishop of San Salvador, who spent his ministry fighting against poverty, social injustice of all kinds, and the abuses of power by the rulers of the day. In 1980 he too was gathered with fellow worshipers celebrating mass when he was gunned down by assassins committed to the kingdom of the world. Or Brother Roger, the founder of the Taizé community, who was stabbed to death in 2005 while he led evening prayer. Or the mass shooting that took place at Emanuel African Methodist Episcopal Church in Charleston in 2015 during a prayer service.

In this garden, Jesus is attacked from all sides; the secular political rulers and the religious rulers (who are also political rulers in their own right) collude to destroy him (in fact, only John mentions the Roman soldiers). Ironically, they come in the dark (remember 3:19–21 and 13:30?), bringing two forms of light to extinguish the Light of the World. And weapons. Always weapons, ready for the violent option.

Jesus does not cower. Instead he confronts the powers with Power. He makes them answer the question that he wants us all to answer: "Whom are you seeking?" When they answer, Jesus delivers another theophany, a manifestation of God by saying, "I am" (*egō eimi*). In case the duller reader doesn't understand that this is a theophany, the author shows the opponents overcome by the majesty that knocks them off of their feet literally. He repeats the question, they repeat their answer, and he repeats his response. By means of this double exchange, Jesus shows that he is simultaneously *both* human and divine, Jesus of Nazareth and God. The phrase *egō eimi* in Greek can be translated "I am" or "I am he." In the first exchange, the author plays on the former. In the second, he shows the equation.

Just as he promised in 17:12, Jesus protects his followers. Peter misses the point; seduced by the strategies of the kingdoms of this world, he resorts to expedient violence. Jesus quickly and decisively once again contrasts the sword with the cup, the will of the powers that be with the will of God, calling us all to choose the latter.

Scene 2: Jesus before a High Priest, Part 1

The camera now switches scenes, as the authorities first take Jesus to Annas (who had previously been the high priest 6–15 CE), Caiaphas's father-in-law. The author expects you to have read everything before this and to recall Caiaphas's ironic words from 11:50. As benefactors of Jesus' obedience, we know that, in fact, it *was* better for Jesus to die for the people. But Caiaphas didn't mean it that way. He speaks the truth while contesting the Truth—thus the irony.

Scene 3: Peter's First Denial

The camera now switches away from Jesus and Annas and watches Peter and another disciple "follow" (a theologically weighted word)

Jesus. Well, almost. Actually, only the other disciple follows. Peter remains an outsider for now. It's worth noting that the other disciple is known to the high priest; so he is immediately granted access. Who is this disciple? Why is the disciple not named? What is the relationship between that disciple and the high priest?

Given the chance to profess his faith in the "I am," Peter replies "I am *not*" when asked if he's a follower. Two words from Jesus, *egō eimi*, contrasted with two words from Peter, *ouk eimi*.

What a difference one word can make!

Hold in your mind the image of the charcoal fire; Peter is warming himself as he stands by it and against Jesus. It becomes important later in the story.

Scene 4: Jesus before a High Priest, Part 2

Now the camera takes us back to Jesus before Annas again. Verse 19 is confusing because it refers to Annas as the high priest when, in actuality, Caiaphas is the high priest (see v. 24; he was high priest 18–36/7 CE). Annas still clearly holds some power, but the title is being used merely in an honorific way. It's similar to the way Americans continue to refer to presidents with that title, even when they are technically former presidents.

Just as in the garden, the authorities try to control Jesus. Once again Jesus refuses to submit to their system and speaks his truth with confidence, come what may. The questioned becomes the questioner. Once again he is treated violently. Remember 1:11 and the fate of Lady Wisdom; she speaks truth, but human beings tend to embrace foolishness—and worse, evil.

Having no good answer, Annas sends Jesus to Caiaphas.

Scene 5: Peter's Second and Third Denials

The camera shifts back to Peter, and the scene virtually repeats itself: Peter is warming himself; he is questioned; he utters the fateful "I am not." Finally, Malchus's relative questions Peter. This time, we don't even hear Peter's own voice; the author just tells us that Peter denies that he has been with Jesus. The cock crows. The image fades out.

Act 2: Judging the Judge: The Trial of Jesus

What makes for a good king? We don't have kings in America, so maybe that question doesn't grip you (though, judging by the number of us captivated by television shows like *Game of Thrones* and *Once upon a Time*, maybe it does). Kings aside, it feels as if we are always in an election year; so we at least regularly ponder, "What makes for a good leader?"

John's trial scene is quite different from that of the Synoptics. So you may for the moment want to lay the Synoptic accounts aside and immerse yourself in the flow and shape of John's narrative, without distraction. John intentionally and dramatically arranges the trial of Jesus before Pilate into eight scenes, punctuated by Pilate's egress to meet "the Jews" and his ingress to interact with Jesus. Each scene—and the whole trial—centers on kingship.

The issue of Jesus' kingship is raised already in chapter 6. After he satisfies the bellies of the five thousand, they try to seize him and force him to be king, but Jesus slips away. His authority as king originates not from this world but from God, and his kingdom has to do with the reign of love, not political expediency aimed at personal aggrandizement. He knows that we tend to enslave ourselves to cynical rulers, for whom power and coercion are synonyms, so long as they satisfy our bellies and require no sacrifice. Jesus also already knows that later in the story the people of God will cry out, with the most devastating irony, "We have no king but Caesar!" (19:15, KJV). And how!

Camera ready?

Scene 1: Jesus Accused (18:28–32)

Jesus is brought from Caiaphas to the praetorium, where Pilate conducts the business of Caesar's empire. The fact that this is pagan, Roman space is emphasized by the use of that Roman word twice. The Jewish authorities who led Jesus there are painstakingly careful to distinguish themselves from the pagan Romans, careful not to enter that physical space lest they be defiled by it. "We serve King God, not King Caesar," they try to say by their actions. But do they? The whole trial narrative is rife with irony.

Since they can't go in, Pilate *goes out* to them. Jesus is inside. Jesus is charged with doing evil. Given the ensuing conversation around kingship, we may surmise that they are hinting at treason or sedition.

Scene 2: The Nature of Jesus' Kingship (18:33–38a)

Returning from asking Jesus' accusers about the charge against him, Pilate *goes in* to the praetorium and questions Jesus about the nature of his kingship. We know from the historical record that Pilate was a brutal man. Assignment to the boondocks of Palestine was not part of his ambitious political career plans. Pilate tries to dismiss "the Jews," but they persist. So he comes to investigate whether Jesus is a political threat to Rome: Are you the King of the Jews? Rather than answer Pilate, Jesus becomes the interrogator and judge in this trial. Pilate is not as in control as he pretends to be (worldly rulers never are), and Jesus knows it (see their exchange in 19:10–11).

In response to Jesus' question, Pilate declares, "I'm not a Jew, am I?" Of course he's not, quite the opposite: he's a Roman representing the arm of the empire that is oppressing Jesus' own people, the Jews. But insofar as John sometimes uses the term "the Jews" as a collective character representing opposition to Jesus, the irony becomes thick. John 1:11 declares, "He came to what was his own, and his own people did not accept him." As Pilate remains opposed to Jesus and entirely uninterested in truth for truth's sake, he does in fact become indistinguishable from those in 1:11 who act out their rejection by handing Jesus over to Pilate.

In verse 36, Jesus responds, in a way, to Pilate's king question. But Jesus does not crow about being a king; rather, he immediately speaks not about himself but about his community, calling it a kingdom (some modern interpreters prefer the word "kindom" to get away from hierarchical, monarchical language). Here he contrasts himself with Pilate:

- Pilate uses power and authority for selfish ends, with no concern for the building of community, and certainly not a community guided by love and truth. Pilate hoards power and lords it over people, even to the point of destroying them, on a cross or otherwise. Jesus empowers others and uses his authority to wash

the feet of those he leads. He spends his life on them, every last ounce of it; he gives his life to bring life.
- Pilate's rule brings terror, even in the midst of "peace" (the so-called *Pax Romana*). Jesus' rule brings peace, even in the midst of terror (14:27; 16:33; 20:19–26).
- Pilate's followers imitate him by using violence to conquer and divide people by race, ethnicity, and nations. Jesus' followers put away the sword in order to invite and unify people, as Jesus does when he says, "And I, when I am lifted up from the earth, will draw all people to myself" (12:32).
- Pilate's authority originates from the will of Caesar and is always tenuous. Jesus' authority originates from the will of God and is eternal.

Jesus places all of this choice conversation material before Pilate, but Pilate hears only Jesus' possible threat to his own authority: "So you *are* a king?" Jesus again pushes deeper to the heart of the matter; this is the trial of the ages. Truth itself is on trial, and Jesus is the star witness. Will Pilate side with truth or cynicism? What about us?

Scene 3: The Jews Choose Barabbas over King Jesus (18:38b–40)

Pilate *goes out* to "the Jews." He offers to release Jesus, mocking the Jews by calling him "King of the Jews" to get under their skin. Ironically, they choose to save an actual political criminal, Barabbas. The people reject the king for a bandit (see 10:1).

Scene 4: The Coronation of Jesus as King (19:1–3)

Pilate *goes in* and has Jesus flogged. Ironically, Jesus is crowned King of the Jews by Roman soldiers. What looks like a moment of defeat is actually the coronation of the true king. As usual, those in power use verbal and physical violence to degrade their prisoner.

Scene 5: The First Presentation of Jesus as King (19:4–7)

Pilate *goes out* to say for a second time that he finds no case against Jesus. That has not stopped him from torturing Jesus for no reason, fulfilling 15:25—"they hated me without a cause" (itself an allusion to Ps. 69:4). Same stuff, different century. Jesus is presented to the people dressed ironically as a king. Pilate sees in him only a "human being": "Behold the human being." If you've done the Stations of the Cross, you will recognize Pilate's statement in the form "Behold the Man." But the Greek text does not say "man" here (that would be *anēr*); it says "human being" (*anthrōpos*). The author is once again playing off of the word for human being. Those who don't fully understand Jesus yet (or ever) see only a human being. Those who do see a prophet, their Lord, and God.

The chief priests and police call for crucifixion and modify the charge: Jesus *claimed* to be the Son of God. See the irony? They don't know the half of it. Not only did he claim to be; he *is*. Furthermore, it's worse than they think: he is equal to God.

Scene 6: Jesus' Authority as King and Son of God Is Revealed (19:8–11)

Pilate *goes in* to question and intimidate Jesus, waving the vast power of the state in front of Jesus' eyes. As usual, Jesus relativizes the powers of this world. They may be strong, but they are not ultimate. They are temporary, not eternal. They rely on terror, not peace. Jesus draws upon the very Peace he promises his disciples then, as now, and continues to speak the truth, come what may.

Scene 7: The Second Presentation of Jesus as King (19:12–16a)

Pilate *goes out* and yet again tries to release Jesus. "The Jews" now bring Caesar into it and overtly make the charge sedition. When it was just an interreligious, theological argument between Jews, Pilate couldn't care less.

Now he presents Jesus for a second time, and again the call for crucifixion rings out. And then the ultimate irony. The very group that was so careful to keep themselves from defilement by not entering the pagan space, by showing the priority of King God over King Caesar, now pledges sole allegiance to King Caesar. It can happen in any country in any century.

The ironic blurring of juridical and political roles is a favorite technique of John's. In 19:13, for example, the text indicates that Pilate "brought Jesus outside and sat [him] on the judge's bench." The way the verb is used here, it's not clear whether Pilate or Jesus is sitting on the judge's bench. But it is clear to us who the real judge is.

Scene 8: Jesus Is Exalted on the Cross and Reigns as King of the Jews (19:16b–22)

The contest between Pilate and "the Jews" about Jesus' kingship continues. For wicked fun, Pilate puts up a mocking placard: "Jesus of Nazareth, King of the Jews." He's being cynical by posting it in three languages, showing the might and breadth of the Roman Empire. But you and I know, because we've read chapter 4, that it's entirely appropriate for the Savior of the whole world to be announced in multiple languages. The joke, of course, is actually on Pilate and Caesar. At the end of the day, it always is.

In the end, Pilate crucifies the Truth. While the Word hangs on a cross in agony, Pilate and the chief priests agonize over words. The sign announces Jesus as the King of the Jews. Pilate has unwittingly announced the truth. There on the cross the King is crowned, not with diamonds or a laurel wreath but with thorns. And from that lofty height, he births the church (19:25–27), his ally in announcing the truth: Loving Truth wins. Over and over again. Long live the King.

Act 3: Spotlight on the Crucifixion

Watching the crucifixion scene in John is quite different from watching it in the Synoptics. I want to zoom in on a few details to draw your attention to them. First, while in the Synoptics Jesus dies alone, with the disciples having entirely fled and the women looking on from a distance, in John there are numerous loved ones at the foot of the cross. Do we have an abundance of Marys there or not? Are there three women or four? Jesus' mother is there, but she is never named in John. Jesus' aunt is there. Is she the same as Mary, the wife of Clopas? That would make both sisters named Mary, it seems. And for the very first time in the story we see Mary Magdalene. Jesus establishes the church as a household of fictive kin. What do

I mean by this? Notice that from the cross Jesus says to his mother, "Woman, behold your son." And to the Beloved Disciple he says, "Behold your mother." The Beloved Disciple and Jesus's mother are not biologically related; they are *Jesus* related. No longer is biology a primary category. Rather, those who seek to follow Jesus become our primary family members, our "real" (rather than merely biological) kin. Biology is incidental; Christian community is intentional.

Second, Jesus remains in control of the unfolding drama, even on the cross. After establishing the church, he next says, "I thirst." He says it for symbolic reasons, specifically to fulfill Psalm 69:21, Psalm 22:15, or both. He then announces, "It has been completed" (19:30, my trans.). It is important to note that in Greek, the verb tense called the perfect indicates action completed in the past with continuing effect into the present. That is the tense used here. What Jesus has been saying throughout the Gospel has now come true: he was sent to do the work God gave him to do, and he has completed it. We are all, to this day, the beneficiaries.

Third, verse 30 declares the keeping of another promise, namely, the giving of the Spirit. English translations get this wrong, probably because they have the Synoptics in mind when translating this passage. It gets translated as a way of saying "Jesus died." But the Greek says Jesus "bestowed the Spirit." Greek words are not capitalized; that's a decision of your translator (in this case, me). Throughout the Gospel, Jesus has promised the Spirit once he departs. Here, on the cross, he establishes the church and bestows the Spirit. The scene will be repeated in a different iteration in the next chapter, when he makes the same move with the disciples who are hiding out in a locked room in fear. The way time works in John is more poetic than literal. Remember the constant reference to "the hour"? It's best to think of the activity from the cross to the end as all one moment for John. After all, isn't that how eternity works?

Fourth, only in John does a soldier pierce Jesus' side with a spear. Blood and water come out. People have found a number of different meanings in this detail. It may be a way to highlight Jesus' true physical humanity (some would argue the same for the "I thirst" statement). Others take a sacramental view, connecting the blood with the Eucharist/Lord's Supper and the water with baptism. Recall 7:38: "Let anyone who believes in me come and drink! As Scripture says,

'From his belly/womb/stomach [*koilia*] shall flow streams of living water'" (my trans.).[1] Perhaps it is all of the above. What meaning do you find in this detail?

Fifth, while Joseph of Arimathea appears in all of the burial accounts, only in John does Nicodemus accompany him. Interpreters weigh in differently on Nicodemus's weighty load. Does he bring so much myrrh and aloes because he "gets it," like Mary in chapter 12, who is effusive with the nard? Or does the hyperbolic hundred pounds signify that he doesn't expect Jesus to arise? Does the author mention Nicodemus's night moves in order to highlight that Nicodemus will always be a shady figure, or does it indicate his former self? Here he is acting before sunset, taking a risk to be associated with Jesus when his disciples are nowhere in sight. What is your own take on Nicodemus, given all that you now know at this point in the story?

Fade to black.

Questions for Reflection

1. What is the proper relationship between Christians and their host culture?
2. Do you find it easy to stick to the truth as you know it, come what may? What circumstances make you waver?
3. You may find it a useful exercise to compare John with the Synoptics here, not to "fix" any of them, but to see how each handles this part of Jesus' life. Questions you might consider:

   a. How does the trial work?
   b. What's the accusation?
   c. How does Jesus respond?
   d. Before whom does he stand trial?
   e. What is Pilate's role?
   f. Why does Jesus die?
   g. Who's at the cross?
   h. What else is significant?

1. It's unclear in the Greek whether the "his" refers to Jesus or to the believer. I think that's intentional on the author's part.

Chapter 14

In the End: Magdalene

John 20:1–18

She arrives late in the story, but once she does, Mary Magdalene takes center stage. Last at the cross, first at the tomb. Charter member of the first church in existence—the one started by Jesus as he hung on the cross and gifted his followers with each other and the Holy Spirit. The first person to encounter the risen Lord, all by herself, and in Christian history the first preacher of the resurrection. Sent by Jesus to proclaim his resurrection to the other disciples, she is the Apostle to the Apostles.

In Christian history, she is maligned by some, adored by others. A pop-culture icon, appearing in books (such as Dan Brown's *The Da Vinci Code*), every Jesus movie (such as *Jesus Christ Superstar* and *Jesus of Montreal*), paintings, and music.

I have written about Mary Magdalene in extensive detail elsewhere. Part of my ongoing task involves correcting erroneous "knowledge" about her.[1] Suffice it to say that nowhere in Scripture does she anoint Jesus; she is not a prostitute or sexually suspect in any way. It's time to put to rest the salacious fantasy of long silky hair, bright blue eye shadow and a jingly belly-dancing skirt. I love *Jesus Christ Superstar* more than most people (my initials are even

1. "Introducing the Real Mary Magdalene," in *Teaching the Bible*, Society of Biblical Literature, http://www.sbl-site.org/assets/pdfs/TBv2i8_ClarkSolesMagdalene.pdf. This article appears in a modified form in Jaime Clark-Soles, *Engaging the Word: The New Testament and the Christian Believer* (Louisville, KY: Westminster John Knox Press, 2010). See also "Mary Magdalene: Beginning at the End," in *Character Studies in the Fourth Gospel: Narrative Approaches to Seventy Figures in John*, ed. Steven A. Hunt, D. Francois Tolmie, and Ruben Zimmermann, Wissenschaftliche Untersuchungen zum Neuen Testament (Tübingen: Mohr Siebeck, 2013) 626–40.

JCS) and belt out (however off-key) "I Don't Know How to Love Him" with passion, but that woman is a figment of the imagination; she is not the Mary Magdalene who appears in Scripture. If you are confused, know that, on the one hand, it's not your fault. You have been fed this misinformation for centuries from the highest offices of the church. Take Pope Gregory, who, in *Homily 33* (dated to 591 CE) took interpretive matters into his own misguided hands: "She whom Luke calls the sinful woman, whom John calls Mary [of Bethany], we believe to be the Mary from whom seven devils were ejected."[2] On the other hand, while our poor sixth-century ancestors had no way to fight back, since they didn't have access to the Bible (or much education) except through church officials, we modern Christians have no excuse for tolerating gross misrepresentations of the details of the biblical texts.

And even now the error has been codified in our everyday language. Take this definition found on A.Word.A.Day, a site managed by Anu Garg. The entry is as follows:

> maudlin
>
> PRONUNCIATION: (MAWD-lin)
>
> MEANING: adjective: Overly sentimental.
>
> ETYMOLOGY: After Mary Magdalene, a Biblical character who was a follower of Jesus. In medieval art she was depicted as a penitent weeping for her sins (she washed the feet of Jesus with her tears) and her name became synonymous with tearful sentimentality.
>
> The name Magdalene means "of Magdala" in Greek and is derived after a town on the Sea of Galilee. The name Magdala, in turn, means "tower" in Aramaic. So here we have a word coined after a person, who was named after a place, which was named after a thing.
>
> In an allusion to her earlier life, Mary Magdalene's name has sprouted another eponym, magdalene, meaning a reformed prostitute.[3]

2. *Homily 33* is found in *Homiliarum in evangelia*, Lib. II, *Patrologia Latina* 76 (Paris: J.-P. Migne, 1844–1864), cols. 1238–1246.

3. Anu Garg, "Maudlin," Wordsmith.org, http://wordsmith.org/words/maudlin.html.

Ugh. Turning to the work at hand, what does Mary Magdalene do in the Gospel after showing up at the cross? She shows up at the tomb. That's what she does. She shows up. Do we?

She's there all alone. She's not happy, she's unclear about what the future holds, she's bereft; but she's there. Isn't that what faithfulness looks like?

In what follows, I will draw your attention to some important details in this passage. I will compare and contrast Mary with Peter and the Beloved Disciple (who appear in the passage), as well as other characters in the Gospel, and ask where the story connects with our own lives.

Mary Comes to the Tomb (20:1)

Let's stay with our filming exercise. The scene opens with Mary Magdalene all alone at the tomb on a Sunday morning. Let me ask you this: Whom would you *expect* to be at the tomb? Do you find it startling that the first person to arrive on the scene, and early, is a character who was introduced into the narrative a mere thirteen verses earlier? Wouldn't you expect the Beloved Disciple, or Jesus' mother, or really any other character who appeared far earlier in the narrative?

Mary Magdalene is being played off of the obviously missing Peter and the Beloved Disciple. She is the first one to go to the tomb, and she is the first to grasp the resurrection. This is typical for this author, who insists (against the sentiments of his or her own time period and culture) that the foundations of the gospel proclamation rest in large part upon female figures. This is part of the Gospel's insistence that God works in mysterious ways, such that the least expected characters—women—appear as chief agents, witnesses, apostles, catalysts, and evangelists. The same pattern of female trust, insight, and proclamation happens in Cana (2:1–12). The disciples are at the wedding, but it's the mother of Jesus who has some idea of Jesus' power and purpose.

Recall the Samaritan woman in chapter 4, who, in contrast to Nicodemus, beholds Jesus as God and evangelizes her town. She is boldly contrasted with the disciples who, as the camera focuses upon them, adopt a Winnie-the-Pooh stance whereby they sit on a stump distracted by many ponderous thoughts about why Jesus is speaking with a woman and what kind of munchies Jesus might be hoarding (4:33), all the while jabbing their forefingers into their temples chanting, "Think, think, think." Pooh always comes out OK in the end, but the road to enlightenment tends to be more circuitous for him than others; so too for the disciples.

Mary Runs to Peter and the Beloved Disciple (20:2)

Mary runs to announce the empty tomb to Peter and the Beloved Disciple.

Spotlight on Peter and the Beloved Disciple (20:3–10)

While it is clear that Mary returns to the tomb as well, the camera leaves her and zooms in as we watch Peter and "the other disciple" engage the empty tomb. The two have a race. They get there, take a quick look, see some linens and no body, believe that the tomb is empty (just as Mary had said) but have no clue as to why. They say nothing and do not investigate. They simply go back to their own stuff that they were doing before she arrived ("homes" does not appear in the Greek). Maybe they are reminiscing; maybe they are strategizing; maybe they are distracting themselves from their grief by fishing or playing ancient X-Box. At any rate, they leave. They go back to their old life. It's the same thing they do after they experience the risen Christ; they just go back to fishing. More on that later.

Throughout John, we are taught that coming, seeing, abiding, believing, and understanding Scripture's testimony about the identity of Jesus are key markers of good discipleship. To their credit, Peter and the Beloved Disciple do come and see—but that's all. You may argue, "But the text says that the Beloved Disciple 'believed.'" But what exactly does he believe at that moment? Often it is assumed that he believes the central message of the G/gospel, namely, that

Jesus has risen from the dead. But this cannot be accurate, since the text immediately states that "they did not understand." Therefore, the only thing that the Beloved Disciple believes at this point is Mary's testimony about the empty tomb.

From Weeping to Joy (20:11–13)

"Weeping may last for the night, but joy comes with the morning" (Ps. 30:5, my trans.). And oh, what a morning!

Unlike the other disciples, Mary stays. She weeps. She confronts her grief in a raw way, bending over to look directly into the very space that is causing her pain. What could be more difficult? She doesn't run around pretending to be happy or chirping, "It's all good! Jesus is in a better place now. Heaven needed one more angel." She lets the tears flow. And then flow some more. But then an amazing thing happens. Through her tears, not in spite of them, she receives an angelophany, a vision of angels, a mystical vision, a gift from God. Has that, or some version of it, ever happened to you?

When Mary Magdalene weeps, she's in good company. Who else weeps in John? Yes, Jesus. And the fact that Mary Magdalene is a "Mary" who "weeps" outside a "tomb" with a "stone" cannot be lost on the reader of John 11, who watched Mary of Bethany weep for Lazarus. Mary of Bethany and Jesus both weep openly for the loss of their loved one.

The angels ask her, "Woman, why are you weeping?" Without apologizing, without any pomp and circumstance, she states what troubles her. She seems to be quite at home in the company of angels. She doesn't appear to straighten her collar, get a stiff upper lip, or lapse into the Queen's English. She just states the truth about where she is in that moment. In fact, she repeats almost exactly what she said back in verse 2, but this time, it becomes deeply personal (and isn't that the point?). Compare the two statements: "They have taken *the* Lord out of the tomb, and *we* do not know where they have laid him" (v. 2); "They have taken away *my* Lord, and *I* do not know where they have laid him" (v. 13).

The "Turning" Point (20:14–17)

The camera then shifts as Mary sees Jesus, who is in a bodily form that she doesn't recognize. His question, "Woman, why are you weeping?" is exactly identical to that of the angels. Furthermore, it recalls the scene with his mother in chapter 2, the only other place Jesus addresses a person as "woman" (2:4). He then asks a question he asks often in the Gospel of John: "Whom do you seek?" (1:38; 4:27; 18:4, 7).

The text tells us that Mary takes Jesus for the gardener. Certainly as the chapter opens, we find that Mary Magdalene is in a garden (cf. 19:41), but this turns out to be the garden of all gardens! The fact that Mary supposes Jesus to be not *a* gardener but *the* Gardener cues us to think of Genesis and the original garden of Eden. We already saw in verse 1 the statement that it is the *first* day, taking us back to the very beginning of creation (Gen. 1:1ff. and John 1:1–5), the very *first* day with the Creator and a garden and two human beings who are trying to work out personhood, and bodies, and gender and sex and earthliness/fallenness/grief/despair and godliness/redemption/peace/joy. The garden is the beginning, the end, and the beginning again.

Mary boldly asks for help with what she thinks she needs: the body of her dead Jesus. She's gets even more than she is hoping for: the voice of her living Lord. In a Gospel that insists that Jesus knows each and every one of us by name and that we, his sheep, know his voice, it's not surprising that it's when he says her name, "Mary," that she "comes to," out of her fog of grief, and sees the reality of the joy in front of her. Notice this oddity in the text: verse 16 says she "turned." This marks a spiritual revelation on her part: she gets it. It cannot mean that she just physically turns around to face him, because she has already done that in verse 14 (same verb, *strephō*).

Naturally she wants to hang on to Jesus. She wants to go back to the way things were, because she can't imagine how she can experience Jesus even more fully forever by letting go now. I can relate to this. Maybe you can too.

It was March 2007. This would be my last phone call with my friend David Lawson, who had been the Bishop-in-Residence at Perkins School of Theology when I arrived in 2001. He was nearing the end of his life after a long period of illness. By then he was back in Indiana, while I was still in Dallas. We began our phone conversation the way we always did: "Whatcha reading these days?" He said, "You're going to give me a hard time, but I'm reading (a specific scholar)." I said, "Well, it's just that he's dogmatic." He said, "So are you." We laughed. As usual, he was also rereading Philippians, his favorite book in the Bible, which had been "picked out" just for him by his eighth-grade Sunday School teacher back when he and his friends were rascals who would sneak out of church to go get ice cream and slip back in before the end of the service. We explored ideas and swapped stories. He gave good, if challenging, advice (his own Farewell Discourse, if you will). We laughed.

He shared a beautiful story with me about helping his grandson come to terms with his dying, a story that ended with this big burly man, who had grown up working on the railroads but was now bedridden, holding his grandson while his grandson sobbed, repeating the words, "Oh Granddaddy. Oh Granddaddy." I told him that I felt the same way, that I was so deeply sad to know that soon I wouldn't be able to pick up the phone and chat or receive e-mails introducing me to new poetry (he was the first to introduce me to Mary Oliver's "Wild Geese," not to mention Kaylin Haught's "God Says Yes to Me"). He tried to console me, shared with me his peace, his appreciation of the springtime, and reminded me of the resurrection and the fact that he wasn't really leaving me.

I teach a class regularly called "Evil, Suffering, and Death in the New Testament" and publish in that area. I am an ordained minister and seminary professor who preaches and teaches about (and believes in!) resurrection and life everlasting. And I love the Gospel of John for a living. All the same, as he tried to soothe my grief, I pushed back. "You know, I am a Johannine scholar. I have read the story of Mary and Jesus in the garden umpteen times, but I've never *really* understood it until right now. I get it. Mary doesn't want to let him go physically. It's so hard. So you will forgive me for wanting to hang on." I also said to him, "You know what? You have taught me and mentored me so much over these years. And you may be sick and dying, but I am not going to let you boss me about this. I'm sad that you are dying, and you aren't going to talk me out of it." It's surprising how, when someone knows you by name, really knows you, you can be honest and uncensored, and even the rawest experiences can become holy ground. Letting go is soul work.

Notice once again how much touching happens in this Gospel. Bodies matter. The text assumes that Mary Magdalene is already touching Jesus and that it would be natural for her to do so. When he tells her to stop touching him, it's not because he's puritanical or cold but because he knows how the story unfolds and that, for the story to move forward, he must return to his and her God, the original Gardener.

Mary on Mission (20:18)

As he is wont to do, Jesus sends Mary on mission to proclaim the resurrected Lord to Jesus' brothers and sisters. Note that the word here (*adelphous*) is inclusive of males and females. The NRSV normally translates it this way, but here, for some reason, it chooses to limit it to brothers. Such a translation is unfounded and inexplicable; it reflects a preconceived bias that only males were disciples (*mathētēs*), though that is patently not true. One must always be watchful when using an English translation.

What Jesus prayed for in John 17 has now come true: the church is one household, and we share the same relationship with God that Jesus does (v. 17). Notice that (so-called Doubting) Thomas, of all people, will be the first one to express this fact later, in verse 28, when he declares: "My Lord and my God!"

Mary promptly preaches the gospel to the disciples, testifying to her personal encounter of the risen Lord, thus setting them up for their own in the next passage.

Mary Magdalene: Jesus' Angel of the Morning

Literally speaking, Mary is Jesus' angel (*angelos*); she announces (*angellō*) the message. With all due respect to Tim Rice, Helen Reddy, and lovers of *Jesus Christ Superstar* everywhere, it turns out that Mary Magdalene does in fact "know how to love him." She is:

- one of Jesus' sheep whom he calls by name,
- a proactive agent who seeks Jesus,
- one who is rewarded with an angelophany and Christophany because she abides patiently,
- one whose grief is turned to joy at the coming of the risen Lord after he is lifted up,
- one who testifies to the reality of the risen Lord,
- the first character to see and proclaim the risen Christ,
- one who is born from above, that is, not "by means of the will of a husband, but of God" (1:12–13, my trans.),
- an evangelist, and
- one who is obedient to the will of Jesus and, therefore, God.

"Ella's Song," sung by Sweet Honey in the Rock, an all-female African American a cappella group, contains these words:

> I'm a woman who speaks in a voice and I must be heard.
> At times I can be quite difficult, I'll bow to no man's word.[4]

They must have had Mary Magdalene in mind! Why? Because in this passage Mary Magdalene speaks more than anyone else—and boldly. The disciples never speak. Jesus and the angels speak, but Mary is the only solely human character to speak. She speaks far more than the angels (they get only three words in the Greek New Testament). Strikingly, she speaks more words than Jesus himself. (Mary Magdalene speaks forty-three words and Jesus speaks thirty-eight.) This is not new for John. Recall chapter 11, where Jesus' dialogue with Martha and Mary of Bethany leads to both of his greatest revelatory statements, "I am the resurrection and the life. Those who believe in me, even though they die, will live" (11:25) and the robust profession and proclamation of Jesus' identity, "Yes, Lord, I believe that you are the Messiah, the Son of God, the one coming into the world" (11:27). Lazarus never says a word.

Mary Magdalene is the first to testify that the resurrected Jesus Christ is the central fact of human history—no, *cosmic* history. In so doing, she herself has become a central fact of that history. Can you hear her voice?

4. Sweet Honey in the Rock, "Ella's Song," *Breaths*, 1988, soundtrack.

Questions for Reflection

1. What images or aspects of Mary Magdalene's story do you relate to?
2. Do you weep? What or whom do you weep for right now? What feels dead or hopeless to you?
3. What is the greatest loss you have ever known?
4. Why is it disturbing when something is not where you buried it?
5. Have you ever heard God call you by name? When was the last time that happened?
6. How might you pay better attention to the presence of *the* Gardener in your own life?
7. What people or things do we hold onto that we should let go?
8. What does the empty tomb of Jesus of Nazareth mean to you?
9. How do you testify to the presence of God in your life?

Chapter 15

Jesus' Twin Appearances

John 20:19–31

Some Not-Thomas Disciples See the Risen Jesus

What do the disciples do in response to Mary Magdalene's proclamation of the risen Jesus, of abundant life, of a world forever changed and open with possibility? They hide in fear behind locked doors. Sound familiar?

Once again, notice the light/darkness motif. Like the Samaritan woman, Mary Magdalene is a person of the day, the light. Like Nicodemus, the disciples are huddled in darkness. Jesus seeks them out and meets them there, offering them peace in place of fear. He shows them his hands and his side, and they know it's Jesus. It never stops being the case that we have this treasure in clay jars, that we experience the world, both inner and outer, through our bodies. What do you make of the fact that the body of the risen Jesus still carries the marks of lived experience? Certainly, from a doctrinal perspective, it emphasizes that Jesus was really human and his body was essential to his personhood, and that the risen Christ is, in fact, Jesus of Nazareth. But what does it mean for you at a more personal level?

He then reiterates his offer of peace. As far as I'm concerned, he can never remind us enough. He also does to them what he did with Mary Magdalene earlier—he sends them on mission. But Jesus never sends us to do what he asks without equipping us for it. So, just as he bestowed the Spirit on the newly formed church at the foot of the cross (19:31), now he breathes on them with the Holy Pneuma (spirit/breath); you should be reminded of Gen. 2:7: "Then the Lord God formed the earth-creature (*ha-adam*) from the dust of the earth, and breathed into its nostrils the breath of life; and the earth-creature became a living person" (my trans.). He then reminds them that with great power (the Holy Spirit) comes great responsibility (discerning God's confrontation of sin and offer of forgiveness).

Believing Thomas

No doubt you have heard the story of Believing Thomas.

Remember when we first saw him back in 11:16? Jesus was planning to head to Judea to raise Lazarus, and the disciples were trying to talk him out of it, since it was dangerous territory for Jesus. Thomas, whom we called Eeyore, makes his first appearance in the Gospel there when he says in his forthright, resigned if brave statement: "Let us also go, that we may die with him."

Let's first look at the other place he appears, 14:1. There Jesus is talking about his impending death and ascension to heaven. Have you ever had the experience where you're in a group, maybe a Sunday School class or even a conversation in your dining room, and somebody says something—maybe they're talking about world events—and at the end everybody acts as if they know what the person is talking about, but you have no idea? Well, that's what happened here. But instead of just nodding his head, Thomas speaks up and says, "Well, actually, I have no idea what you're talking about." Thomas is a straight shooter, a practical guy. He may not have much imagination or sense of mystery, but he does have an enquiring mind. Thomas asks the tough questions that others are scared or embarrassed to ask. Thomas is a no-nonsense guy, and I can appreciate that. So maybe we shouldn't be so surprised at what happens in John 19: Thomas stays in character.

When Jesus appears to the disciples in the locked room, where's Thomas? The text doesn't say, so you are free to imagine where he is, what he's doing, and what he may be thinking and feeling, based on what you know about Thomas. We don't know where his friends find him, but they tell him the news. And how does Thomas react? Is he overjoyed and comforted? No. He reacts just as the disciples do when Mary tells them the same thing. Are they overjoyed? Do they run out to the garden to find Jesus? No, Jesus has to find them.

Then Thomas makes his dramatic statement: "Unless I see the mark of the nails in his hands and shove my finger into the mark of the nails, and shove my hand into his side, I will absolutely not believe" (20:25, my trans.). The verb is a forceful one (*ballō*), as is the emphatic negative (*ou mē*). Not a simple, "I'll believe it when I see it," He has a lot of conditions. That's another reason I can relate to Thomas. He puts conditions on his faith. Do you? Thomas wants hard evidence, unquestionable eyewitness fact that Jesus is risen. I can't blame him. You know why? Two reasons. First, he's asking to see what all the other disciples already saw. Second, who doesn't love a solid sign in a moment of crisis and vulnerability? No, I can't blame Thomas. So what happens?

Eight days after Thomas makes this pronouncement, his wish comes true. And then some. Jesus appears and speaks directly to Thomas. Now the Bible doesn't tell us that Thomas ever even touched the wounds. I get the feeling that once Thomas got a look and felt the presence of the risen Lord, he probably forgot all of his conditions. The only thing he could spit out was, "My Lord and my God." In other words, the presence of the risen Lord blotted out Thomas's petty skepticisms and puny proofs and arrogant arguments. This was the glory of the risen Lord, and the only appropriate response was to confess him as Lord and God. And that's another reason I like Thomas. He knew when he was beat. He knew there was a time to shut up and bow down. In my eyes, Thomas was blessed, and I'm jealous that he got such a wonderful opportunity.

But you know what Jesus says? He says to Thomas, "Have you believed because you have seen me (reread John 2:23–25 and 4:48 to see that John is quite impatient with those who *need* signs and wonders to believe and follow Jesus)? Blessed are those who have *not* seen and yet have come to believe." That, of course, includes at least the reader of John's Gospel. That's you and me!

In Thomas we see the pattern of Christian discipleship established by John from chapter 1 on. One person encounters Jesus. Then they share their experience with the next person, who may express some reluctance. Then that person experiences Jesus on their own, directly, and becomes convinced about him and then shares the news about Jesus with the next person. Andrew tells Peter. Philip tells

Nathanael. The Samaritan woman tells the townspeople. "Come and see" is the refrain.

With respect to the witness of the resurrected Jesus, Mary Magdalene starts it off. She encounters Jesus, shares the news; the others don't really buy it until they have *their own* experiences so that they can own the experience. They become convinced and then share it with Thomas. Like the other disciples, Thomas doesn't come to the fullest faith until he has his own experience. I say fullest faith, because he already has faith. The text says, "Don't *become* a faithless person" (my trans.).[1] Move from where you are to the *next* level.

Then the story moves through the chain, and you and I are up next. Thomas makes his confession and, through this text, testifies to us. Now what will we do? Will we hang in there with some level of interest and commitment until we encounter Jesus in a way that moves us to the *next* level? What would the next level look like for you, understanding that we are all in very different places?

For the author, the highest level is *living abundantly*. Are we there yet?

In the end, it's not Thomas's doubting that matters; it's his believing. Everybody doubts; not everyone believes. Be a believing Thomas; be awestruck and proclaim with him: "My Lord and my God."

1. For more on this debate, see Francis J. Moloney, *The Gospel of John*, Sacra Pagina 4 (Collegeville, MN: The Liturgical Press, 1998), 539.

Chapter 16

Breakfast at Tiberias, or the Original Breakfast Club

John 21

*H*ave you ever fallen from grace? Or at least asked yourself, "Am I just a pretender when it comes to this Christian faith thing?" If not, I won't judge you. But you may not understand the following story from John 21 as well as the rest of us.[1]

Like all chapters of John, chapter 21 deserves its own book! It's full of endlessly fascinating material that causes you wonder, tickles your imagination, makes you laugh, challenges your soul, breaks your heart, puts it back together again, and just generally takes your breath away. There's not enough time or space (in this book or in a lifetime) fully to answer the question: "What's this chapter *about*?" Let's do a first run through together; by the time we're done, I hope you can name some connections between the story and your life.

Take a look at the disciples. In chapter 20, they experience Jesus' resurrection in a dramatic way. Mary Magdalene has the first encounter with the risen Christ and tells the others. Jesus comes to them, breathes on them, and bestows the Spirit. Then he reappears for Thomas's sake. Astonishing. After all of this mountaintop mystic stuff, surely they're going to abandon their normal lives and run around spreading the gospel to the ends of the earth, risking shipwreck and pirates at every turn! Not so much. In chapter 21, we find them fishing, back to business as usual, back to the same life they'd been leading before Jesus blasted on the scene. You get the feeling

1. I am reminded of Shel Silverstein's little poem "Invitation," which seems fitting here. You will find it easily on the Internet and in Shel Silverstein's *Where the Sidewalk Ends* (New York: Harper and Row, 1974), 9.

that they've lost their verve; for them, transformation is a thing of the past. I imagine they were in the boat looking back on the good old days with a strong sense of nostalgia. Because they're living in the past, they aren't seeking Jesus in the present and aren't expecting him to show up in any way that really matters. *Are we*?

Preliminary Musings

John 21 probably comprises a second ending to John, written later to highlight Peter (remember that in John the Beloved Disciple is the exemplary follower), since eventually Peter becomes the "representative disciple" in the tradition. As the story begins, seven disciples are accounted for. Where are the others? Who exactly are the "two others"? One must be the Beloved Disciple, given verse 7. I am struck this time around by the author's comment that Jesus "manifests" himself again. The word is *phaneroō*, as in "epi*phany*" and theo*phany*. Jesus shows up. It's what he does. Then the author specifies: "This time, he showed up in *this* way." It goes to show that Jesus can show up in innumerable ways, so be on the lookout.

By now you are accustomed to John's patterns, so you notice that while the disciples work in the dark (metaphor, anyone?), they "catch" nothing. But when they come to the light, blessings abound. Jesus, the Light of the World, appears on the shore, on solid ground at daybreak. We know he's in the habit of asking questions that he already knows the answers to, for our sake, so he asks them about their catch. Without him, they have nothing. With him, there is more than enough.

As is typical for John, the Beloved Disciple gets pride of place; not surprisingly, then, he's the first to recognize Jesus. Peter does his Peter thing. Peter is naked (metaphor, anyone?). I find that such a poignant detail. When he sees Jesus, he puts on clothes to jump in the water. Recall Genesis and the way that nakedness and guilt/shame work together in the story of the fall. If chapter 20 with Mary Magdalene is act 1 of the UNfall drama, this is act 2. Peter clothes his nakedness (well, at a physical level) to face his Friend, Savior, Lord, God. As if.

The disciples come ashore. Throughout Scripture water represents chaos (the Flood, Jonah, Leviathan, the Stilling of the Storm), and, like God, Jesus is shown to have the ability to control that water (and presumably the monsters therein; cf. Jesus walking on water in 6:16–21). Take in 21:9. First, they see a charcoal fire there. Remember Peter standing by a charcoal fire as he is denying Jesus three times (18:18)? The "charcoal fire" appears only in these two places in all of Scripture, and it's not accidental. Charcoal fire: site of failure and site of redemption. Theology of place. Do you have such a place in your life?

Jesus is there, ahead of them (and us), with the fire going and the fish and bread cooking. How did he already have fish? He is the Bread from Heaven, as we learned in chapter 6, so we are not surprised by his provision of bread/manna. Every table is his table. He is always there before us. But notice that he instructs them to add what they have to what he has provided. It's a partnership. That's the true spirit of radical hospitality, isn't it? The eucharistic overtones are striking.

Jesus and Peter

Have you ever been present when a conversation between two people turns so intimate that it becomes awkward for you to listen in or stay there? If not, then get ready.

At 21:15, it gets real. After the beautiful reunion and rich breakfast, Jesus gets personal and addresses Peter by name. Over and over again in this Gospel, John insists that Jesus knows you and me by name, down to every last detail of our lives, from our brilliant flashes of insight to our devastating capacity for destruction—not to mention our peculiar penchant for sheer apathy.

Every time I watch this scene in *The Gospel of John* movie I find myself deeply moved.[2] It's just raw. When some people picture this scene, Jesus and Peter are having a private conversation; others imagine it in front of the group. The movie opts for the latter. What do you think?

2. *The Visual Bible: The Gospel of John* (2003). Directed by Philip Saville.

Round 1

The author piles up all the names for Peter: "Jesus said to Simon Peter, 'Simon son of John, do you love (*agapaō*) me more than these?'" It's important to note the ambiguity in the phrase "more than these." The question has been interpreted in very different ways. The Greek allows any of the following:

1. Do you love me more than these other disciples love me? (This assumes, like the movie, that the question is being asked in front of the whole group.)
2. Do you love me more than you love these other people? (This also assumes a group context but doesn't make very much sense.).
3. Do you love me more than you love all of this stuff, this fishing gear, the boat, your regular, workaday life—your comfort zone?

Number three makes far more sense than the other options. Furthermore, given the whole Farewell Discourse, it makes sense to me that Peter's vocation and Christian calling would be worked out *in* community, not separate from it. I think the movie gets it exactly right here (the movie, by the way, had the Johannine scholar Adele Reinhartz as a consultant, so it is an informed interpretation—not perfect, but informed).

Peter answers reflexively, as I imagine we all would: "Yes, Lord, you know that I love (*phileō*) you." Jesus responds: "Feed my lambs." Love is expressed through radical hospitality.

Rounds 2 and 3

Two more times, for a total of three, Jesus asks Peter if he loves him. Two more times, for a total of three, Peter expresses his love for Jesus. Does your heart break for Peter, for yourself, when you watch Jesus push Peter into the space of vulnerability necessary to break Peter open and free him? What looks so painful and intrusive turns out to be restorative and liberating.

What does Peter learn in the process? First, Jesus knows each of us intimately and meets us in our need. The Samaritan woman needed water, so Jesus was Living Water. The folks in chapter 6 needed bread, so Jesus was the Bread from Heaven. Peter denied

Jesus three times, so Jesus let Peter express three times his love for Jesus. And if Peter had denied him a thousand times, then Jesus would have reminded him a thousand times that his *truest* self is the self that loves and follows Christ. The self that is driven by fear, expediency, and bouts of despair is just a sorry defense mechanism.

Second, Jesus always challenges Peter to show his love through service, through radical hospitality. Christians are to feed Christ's flock. Who's in the flock? Everyone, multiple "others" beyond Peter's imagination at this moment in his story (see chap. 10:16). But that will change by the time Peter dies. Can we say the same?

Jesus knows that he can't send Peter out to serve until Peter has understood that he is fully forgiven, loved without condition, released from the paralyzing grip of guilt and/or shame. His story is our story as he moves beyond past failure and present imperfection into the hopeful, confident, future story that God has intended for us all along. "I came that they might have life." Bare minimum life? Only 99.9% life? Not with Jesus. "I came that they might have life, and have it more abundantly" (10:10). Part of Peter's healing involves his commission to serve.

Healing and life were never meant to be something just between me and Jesus. When one is reconciled to Jesus, brought back home to him, one serves—one feeds Jesus' lambs. He doesn't say, "Make them sign a statement of doctrinal purity," or "Make them follow this specific set of rules"; he says, "Feed them." The disciples and Jesus are in partnership. Though the disciples are sad to see him go, Jesus knows if they are going to mature into the servants that God intends, he has to get out of their way so they can do what Jesus called "greater works than I myself have done." That's radical hospitality, radical service, radical partnership.

Peter does, in fact, answer Jesus' call unto death. Apart from James and Judas, the Bible does not report how any of the other earliest disciples died. According to later tradition, Peter was crucified (hence the reference to stretching out Peter's hands) upside down, as he did not consider himself worthy to be crucified in the same way as Jesus.

Love Correction

When I teach chapter 21, the question always arises about the differences between the two Greek verbs used for love, *agapaō* and *phileō*. Here's the layout:

Scene 1
Jesus: "Do you love (*agapaō*) me?"
Peter: "I love (*phileō*) you."

Scene 2 (identical to Scene 1)
Jesus: "Do you love (*agapaō*) me?"
Peter: "I love (*phileō*) you."

Scene 3
Jesus: "Do you love (*phileō*) me?"
Peter: "I love (*phileō*) you."

The argument I encounter goes like this. *Agapaō* (the noun is *agapē*) love is divine, selfless love and is of a higher order than *phileō* (the noun is *philos*, "friend"), which is a lower, self-interested human love. Jesus is operating from a divine *agapē* love, but Peter can only express the lower-order, lesser love. So finally Jesus gives in and just meets Peter where he is, at the level of human love.

The argument is as common as it is wrong. What's more, that argument goes against the entire grain of this Gospel and the doctrine of incarnation. It's Platonic and gnostic and views the earth and all that's in it as a defective, second-rate knock-off copy of the "real" thing that God is keeping out of our reach. But John says that divine love is friendly love and friendly love is divine love (1 John carries on the theme beautifully). In fact, the Gospel of John uses *phileō* often with respect to the way God or Jesus loves; so it makes no sense to separate the earthly and the heavenly love. Reread John 1:14 and John 17. Jesus has obliterated our categories. The stuff of earth *is* the stuff of heaven!! The word became *flesh*. He is the Bread from Heaven. He is the Living Water. We are called and equipped to love exactly as God loves. We have no excuses for anemic expressions of love. Any limitations on the possibilities of divine love here and now are of our own making, a failure of imagination. Is there any worse failure? Whoever invented the expression: "Go big or go home" must have had loving, Jesus style, in mind.

Peter, Starring as Peter, and the Never Ending Story

Lest we submit to flights of fancy as we stand in awe of the final sacrifice that Peter will make on behalf of Jesus, John brings us back to earth to remind us that, though he died far more valiantly and violently than we will, Peter was Peter until the end of his life. After this beautiful, heart-wrenching scene where Peter receives complete forgiveness and a robust commission, what's the first thing Peter does? What he always does. He gets competitive and comparative with his colleague in ministry. Recall that at verse 19 Jesus told Peter, "Follow me." Period. He didn't ask Peter to butt into the callings of anyone else. He gave Peter his job and equipped him to do it. But Peter can't bear it; he has to know where he stands, not just with respect to Jesus (that's already been made clear), but also with respect to the other disciple, Jesus' Beloved. Jesus confronts Peter to say, "What does my relationship with this person have to do with you? I told you to follow me. Do your job." How many of us play the comparison game just the way Peter does? We have a convicting, amazing experience, and then it gets reduced by our need to interpret it through comparative, competitive lenses. We might do well to let Jesus ask his question anew [afresh]: "If (fill in the blank for yourself), what's that to you?"

The beauty of signing on with Christ, among other things, is this: you get to be you, and you being you brings the Creator of this universe, of all universes, deep delight. You learn that nothing you have done makes your life and your future irredeemable. Repeatedly Peter denies Jesus, willingly and willfully alienates himself from the one who knows and loves him best. Not once, I tell you, but *repeatedly*. Peter denies and rejects love, faith, God, loyalty, friendship, and hope and is complicit in the death of an innocent man.

So sure, you and I have said and done some things we wish we hadn't. And you and I fully believe in Easter morning but cry over the personal good Fridays we confront after Easter Sunday. We fall back into old patterns. But always, always, Jesus comes, looks into our eyes and our very souls, and asks us questions that seem obvious, painful, or offensive at first blush but turn out to be the only questions that matter. And as we answer, we move beyond rote response to something like wonder, like comprehension, like transformation, and we are never the same—similar, but not the same. Praise God.

Ending, Part 2

"But there are also many other things that Jesus did; if every one of them were written down, I suppose that the world itself could not contain the books that would be written" (21:25). Having put Peter in his place and done apologetics regarding the death of the Beloved Disciple, John closes by announcing to us that, without a doubt, there is much more other material in circulation that does not make it into John. We know, by reviewing the Synoptics, that this is quite true. So John never intended to tell you "everything that is known about Jesus." Rather, he understands the difference between knowledge for the sake of knowledge and knowledge for the sake of transformation. The Gospel of John has conveyed such knowledge for centuries now; people have, in every generation, in all manner of places and circumstances, encountered the risen Christ through this text. When faced with the choice to flee or to follow, many have found the words of Peter to ring true: "Lord, to whom can we go? You have the words of eternal life. We have come to believe and know that you are the Holy One of God" (6:68–69). Come and see!

Appendix

"The Jews" in the Fourth Gospel

The Problem of Translation

John's Gospel refers seventy-one times in sixty-seven verses to *hoi Ioudaioi*.[1] The phrase appears in every single chapter of John except the Farewell Discourse (chaps. 14–17) and chapter 21. The NRSV usually translates this phrase "the Jews," although the phrase resists facile translation, because it does not mean the same thing each time it occurs. Numerous scholars have suggested various meanings for *hoi Ioudaioi* in the different instances in John, and these have been considered and categorized by Urban von Wahlde.[2]

"The Jews." First, the "national" sense refers to religious, cultural, or political aspects of people. When an event occurs in the time frame described as a festival of *hoi Ioudaioi*, it may be fine to translate it as "the Jews," because indeed the Festival of Sukkot (Booths or Tabernacles), for example, is a Jewish occasion, not a pagan one. Additionally, when Jesus declares to the Samaritan woman that "salvation is from the Jews" (4:22), he invokes the whole ethno-socio-religious history of God's covenant with Abraham and Sarah, Isaac

1. John 1:19; 2:6, 13, 18, 20; 3:1, 22, 25; 4:9 (twice), 22; 5:1, 10, 15, 16, 18; 6:4, 41, 52; 7:1, 2, 11, 13, 15, 35; 8:22, 31, 48, 52, 57; 9:18, 22 (twice); 10:19, 24, 31, 33; 11:8, 19, 31, 33, 36, 45, 54, 55; 12:9, 11; 13:33; 18:12, 14, 20, 31, 33, 35, 36, 38, 39; 19:3, 7, 12, 14, 19, 20, 21 (three times), 31, 38, 40, 42; 20:19.

2. Urban von Wahlde, "The Johannine 'Jews': A Critical Survey," *New Testament Studies* 28 (1982): 33–60; "'The Jews' in the Gospel of John: Fifteen Years of Research (1983–1998)," *Ephemerides Theologicae Lovanienses* 76 (2000): 30–55. See also Joshua D. Garroway, "*Ioudaios*," in *The Jewish Annotated New Testament*, ed. Amy-Jill Levine and Marc Z. Brettler (New York: Oxford University Press, 2011), 524–26.

and Rebekah, and Jacob and Rachel and Leah. This usage is ethically neutral and merely descriptive. Von Wahlde includes the following passages in this category: 2:6, 13; 3:1; 4:9a, 9b, 22; 5:1; 6:4; 7:2; 11:55; 18:20, 35; 19:21a, 40, 42.

"The Judeans." Sometimes, though, it is better to translate *hoi Ioudaioi* as "the Judeans." Von Wahlde calls this the "regional" sense. If one changes the Greek *I* to an English *J* (as we do with Jesus' name), one can practically hear the word "Judea." At times the term is used to designate those who are geographically connected to Judea. This usage also is ethically neutral and merely descriptive and can be found in the following verses: 3:22, 25; 11:8, 19, 31, 33, 36, 45, 54; 12:9, 11; 19:20.

Here is where it begins to get complicated, though, because it is clear that Jesus comes into conflict with the leaders of his own tradition, whose symbolic (and literal) seat of power was located in Jerusalem, which, of course, is in Judea. As the three-year ministry of Jesus is narrated, notice that Galilee is a safe haven of sorts for Jesus, whereas each time that he goes to Jerusalem (or even contemplates it), ominous music begins to play in the background. In 1:19 we read: "This is the testimony given by John when *hoi Ioudaioi* sent priests and Levites from Jerusalem to ask him, 'Who are you?'" One might argue that this should be translated as "the Judeans," since the party comes from Judea.

"The Religious Authorities." The example from 1:19, however, raises another translation possibility. It is not everyone in Judea who sends priests and Levites; it is patently the religious authorities. The same is true in 7:13, and in both cases it would be best to translate *hoi Ioudaioi* as "the religious authorities." They are not the only religious leaders, though, as even 1:19 makes clear with the mention of priests and Levites. There are also high priests, rulers, and Pharisees. This brings us to von Wahlde's third category, which he designates the "Johannine use" of the word; most instances of the phrase *hoi Ioudaioi* fall into this category, so it is worth explicating, if briefly.

First, in these instances, the term does not have the national meaning, since these "Jews" are distinguished from other characters in the narrative who are also Jewish in the national sense. In other words, taken in a literal ethnic or religious sense, it makes no sense to translate these instances as "the Jews," because that does not distinguish them from anyone else in the Gospel: apart from the centurion and Pilate, everyone in the narrative is Jewish (even the Greeks in chap. 12 may be Greek Jews), both those who believe in Jesus and those who do not. Second, this usage is characterized by hostility toward Jesus. Passages that depict hostile or skeptical religious authorities include 1:19; 2:18, 20; 5:10, 15, 16, 18; 7:13, 15; 9:18, 22a, 22b; 18:12, 14, 36; 19:38; 20:19. Third, in these instances, the authorities labeled "the Jews" think and act en masse: "they represent a single undifferentiated reaction."[3] This use includes 2:18, 20; 7:35.

Religious Authorities or the Common People? Another issue that always arises in the debate about *hoi Ioudaioi* in John is that, after one has moved through the national and regional meanings (which are ethically neutral) and has extracted the passages that refer rather clearly to religious authorities, one still has a batch of verses to address. With those, it is less clear whether the author has in view the religious authorities or the common people. This becomes even further complicated because sometimes the author blurs the line between *hoi Ioudaioi* and the "world" (*kosmos*). The "world" is another complex character in John's Gospel, sometimes believing and sometimes not. "He was in the world, and the world came into being through him; yet the world did not know him" (1:10). Some interpreters conflate "the [unbelieving] Jews" with "the [unbelieving] world." Such a move is not helpful.

For our purposes, one of which includes reading the New Testament ethically, trying to determine which instances might refer to the common people instead of the authorities is not productive and can, in fact, lead to a reasoning that results in a seemingly "partial" anti-Semitism: "Well, it is not Jews per se who are to be maligned, but just their leaders; or maybe just the Jews who did not accept Jesus; or maybe just the Jews who do not accept him now." Faulty logic quickly becomes deadly logic. That said, with respect to the "debatable" instances, von Wahlde argues that, with two exceptions (6:41, 52), they likely refer still to "the religious authorities" rather than "the common people." These are 7:1, 11; 8:22, 48, 52, 57; 10:24, 31, 33; 11:8; 13:33; 18:31, 38; 19:7, 12, 14, 31.

We have now accounted for all of the occurrences of *hoi Ioudaioi*

3. Von Wahlde, "The Johannine 'Jews,'" 47.

and shown the variety of meanings and the problems in attempting a reasonable translation in each instance. Two further observations should be made. First, because John's passion narrative has been a particularly thorny text with respect to Christian anti-Semitism, it may be worth noting that even there varieties in meaning inhere. The "Johannine sense" of *hoi Ioudaioi* appears in the following, according to von Wahlde: 18:12, 14, 31, 36; 19:12, 14, 31. The following use one or another of the other senses discussed earlier: 18:20, 33, 35, 39; 19:3, 19, 20, 21a, 21b, 21c, 40, 42.

Untranslated. Second, regarding the meaning of the seventy-one occurrences of *hoi Ioudaioi*, there is actually a surprising level of general agreement among scholars about the "Johannine uses." The following seven, however, remain the most contested: 3:25; 8:31; 10:19; 11:54; 18:20; 19:20, 21. So riddled with difficulties is this translation issue that many scholars simply leave the phrase untranslated in those cases. Several authors of the essays in these volumes have made precisely that choice.

The Importance of Context

The Fourth Gospel evinces numerous tensions within itself, obvious literary seams, responses that do not answer the question posed, and so on. There are apparent strata, and scholars posit a lengthy and complicated composition history. Let us take a moment to sort out at least three of these strata chronologically.

1. Jesus of Nazareth is born, conducts his ministry, and dies at the hands of the Roman governor Pontius Pilate in about 30 CE.
2. Post-Easter, Jesus' disciples preach publicly about Jesus' identity, words, and deeds.
3. These oral traditions are committed to writing and eventually are drawn together into the narrative we know as the Gospel of John. Tension with the parent tradition remains high as the community discerns its identity vis-à-vis that tradition.
4. Sometime after the composition of the Fourth Gospel, the Epistles of John are penned, reflecting a later stage of the community. The issues now center on internal church conflict among the leaders, apostasy, and docetic Christology.

At the time of Jesus, the temple in Jerusalem is still standing, and numerous varieties of Judaism exist. The power of the Sadducees is temple-based; thus, when the temple is destroyed in 70, they fade from power. The Zealots, Sicarii, and the Fourth Philosophy are nationalists who oppose Roman occupation and favor civil war. The Essenes are a reformist, ascetic sect residing primarily at Qumran near the Dead Sea. The nationalists and the Essenes are decimated by the Roman army in the war of 66–70. The Pharisees are Torah-based teachers whose power derives from their ability to interpret the law—kind of a cross between lawyers and Bible scholars. When the temple is destroyed, they are the ones best positioned to assume leadership. The destruction of the temple effectively ends the period known as Second Temple Judaism and makes way for rabbinic Judaism, the kinds of Judaism that perdure to this day.

The original Johannine community consisted of Jews who worshiped in synagogues with their fellow Jews; they were Christian Jews because they believed that Jesus was the Messiah. Claiming that "the" or "a" Messiah had come was certainly not foreign to first- and second-century varieties of Judaism. John of Gischala in the first century and Simon Bar Kochba in the second were declared messiahs. This was not grounds for dismissal from the Jewish community. So what happened? It is impossible to say with certainty, but clearly the Johannine community began to experience conflict with its parent tradition. The author of the Fourth Gospel claims that the members who made up John's community were put out of the synagogue, *aposynagōgos* (a word unknown in early Jewish or Christian literature apart from John 9:22; 12:42; 16:2), due to their high Christology, perhaps even confessing Jesus as God. It is clear that a full confession of the identity of Jesus as defined by John led to extremely painful conflict between the parent tradition and the sect that formed as a result of their expulsion from the synagogue.

According to J. Louis Martyn,[4] John can be read as a two-level drama. First, there is the story of the historical Jesus, what happened "back then." Second, there is the reality that the Johannine community is experiencing near the end of the first century, sixty to seventy

4. J. Louis Martyn, *History and Theology in the Fourth Gospel, Revised and Expanded*, New Testament Library (Louisville, KY: Westminster John Knox Press, 2003).

years after Jesus' death and twenty to thirty years after the temple has been destroyed; the Pharisees (not the Sadducees) are in power, and the synagogue (not the temple) is the seat of power for the religious authorities. The story of the Johannine community living in the late first century gets retrojected onto the story of Jesus and the first disciples.

For example, when one is reading in chapter 9 the story of the blind man being persecuted and put out of the synagogue, unsupported by his parents, one should imagine a Johannine Christian who is openly professing faith in Christ and being persecuted by members of the parent tradition. The story is anachronistic, because the Pharisees and the synagogue were not such centers of power in Jesus' own day; the Sanhedrin and temple were. It is also anachronistic because no one could give a confession of Jesus as Lord (as the blind man does), Son of God, God (as Thomas does), Messiah, Son of Man, and more until *after* the passion, resurrection, sending of the Paraclete, and return of Jesus to God. In other words, the story could not have happened historically the way it is narrated. One should therefore be careful about making historical assumptions based on texts that have a different rhetorical aim. Certainly the text caricatures anyone who opposes Jesus, the hero of the narrative. The Pharisees are not excused from the Fourth Evangelist's lampooning.

While certain aspects of this reconstruction have recently been contested,[5] important conclusions and warnings can nevertheless be drawn from it. First, the Fourth Gospel reflects an intra-Jewish debate, not a debate between "Christians" and "Jews"; they are all Jews. This is the way sects develop. The Johannine community makes sense of itself as a Jewish community in categories drawn from the Hebrew Bible and Jewish markers of all kinds. Remembering this is crucial when reading this text. Those who choose to ignore the concrete social setting of the New Testament will find it easy to justify anti-Semitism by drawing on John. His violent, seething language about "the Jews" has been used and still is used to charge Jews with all sorts of wickedness.

5. See the work of Adele Reinhartz, for example: *Befriending the Beloved Disciple: A Jewish Reading of the Gospel of John* (New York/London: Bloomsbury Academic, 2002); and "John," in *The Jewish Annotated New Testament*, 152–96.

Second, remember that the Gospel is a story and follows narrative conventions, including characters drawn for symbolic purposes, conflict that the hero must overcome, and so on. It is not a historical rendering, and it takes great poetic license in its depiction of history. Interpreters will be able to understand that only when they learn about the historical context from historical sources that, happily, scholars have provided in abundance.

The Insidious Problem of Anti-Semitism

Easter has always been a potentially dangerous time for Jews, as Christians accuse them of being guilty of deicide, of being Christ-killers, and, thanks to John 8, of being murderous children of the devil. In a post-Shoah world, it is ethically incumbent upon all Christians, especially those who preach and teach, to address and to battle anti-Semitism. There are at least three ways that the Gospel of John may fuel anti-Semitism. We have already addressed the first problem: the repeated use of the phrase *hoi Ioudaioi* in primarily pejorative ways.

The second problem is Johannine dualism. It begins already in chapter 1, where "grace and law" and "Jesus and Moses" are presented as opposites: "From his fullness we have all received, grace upon grace. The law indeed was given through Moses; grace and truth came through Jesus Christ" (1:16–17). Other dualistic categories include light and darkness, truth and falsehood, life and death, God the Father and Satan the father, above and below, not of this world and of this world. Jesus and the disciples are associated with all of the good categories; "the Jews" are primarily associated with the negative trait in each pair.

This contributes to a third problem that arises in the Fourth Gospel: the use of typology in a way that leads to Christian supersessionism.[6] Jesus is depicted as like, but superior to, numerous Old Testament figures, including Moses (chaps. 1, 5, 6), Jacob (1:51; chap. 4), Abraham (chap. 8), and Woman Wisdom herself. Jewish

6. Supersessionism is a theological claim that Christianity supersedes or replaces Judaism in God's plan of redemption. Sometimes it is called fulfillment or replacement theology.

symbols and rituals now find their fulfilled meaning only in Jesus: his incarnation is a tabernacle (1:14); his body is now the temple (chap. 2); he is the bread from heaven celebrated in the Passover; he is the Passover lamb (which is why he dies a day earlier in John than in the Synoptics); he is the King of the Jews. He has fulfilled or replaced everything worthwhile in Judaism. In this way, John may be accused of being anti-Jewish, if not anti-Semitic. Helpful is the following from the Jewish Johannine scholar Adele Reinhartz:

> It must be emphasized that the Gospel is not anti-Semitic in a racial sense, as it is not one's origins that are decisive but one's beliefs. Nevertheless, it has been used to promote anti-Semitism. Most damaging has been John 8:44, in which Jesus declares that the Jews have the devil as their father. . . . While John's difficult rhetoric should not be facilely dismissed, it can be understood as part of the author's process of self-definition, of distinguishing the followers of Jesus from the synagogue and so from Jews and Judaism. This distancing may have been particularly important if the ethnic composition of the Johannine community included Jews, Samaritans, and Gentiles. This approach does not excuse the Gospel's rhetoric, but it may make it possible for readers to understand the narrative's place in the process by which Christianity became a separate religion, to appreciate the beauty of its language, and to recognize the spiritual power that it continues to have in the lives of many of its Christian readers.[7]

The authors and editors of the two John volumes of *Feasting on the Gospels* have worked diligently to bear such convictions in mind as they worked through this rich and complex Gospel to offer preachers, teachers, Bible study leaders, and interested Christian readers guidance through the thicket of language and images that historically have divided Christians from Jews and frequently resulted in Christian violence against Jews.

7. Reinhartz, "John," 156.

Selected Bibliography

Anderson, Paul. *The Riddles of the Fourth Gospel.* Minneapolis: Fortress, 2011.

Black, Kathy. *A Healing Homiletic: Preaching and Disability.* Nashville: Abingdon, 1996.

Callahan, Allen Dwight. "John." In *True to Our Native Land: An African American New Testament Commentary*, edited by Brian K. Blount. 186–212. Minneapolis: Fortress, 2007.

Carter, Warren. "'The Blind, Lame, and Paralyzed' (John 5:3): John's Gospel, Disability Studies, and Postcolonial Perspectives." In *Disability Studies and Biblical Literature*, edited by Candida R. Moss and Jeremy Schipper. 129–50. New York: Palgrave Macmillan, 2011.

Clark-Soles, Jaime. *Engaging the Word.* Louisville, KY: Westminster John Knox Press, 2010.

———. "'The Jews' in the Fourth Gospel." In *Feasting on the Gospels—John, Volume 1: A Feasting on the World Commentary,* edited by Cynthia A. Jarvis and E. Elizabeth Johnson. xi-xiv. Louisville, KY: Westminster John Knox Press, 2015.

———. "Mary Magdalene: Beginning at the End." In *Character Studies in the Fourth Gospel: Narrative Approaches to Seventy Figures in John,* edited by Steven A. Hunt, D. Francois Tolmie, and Ruben Zimmermann. 626–40. Wissenschaftliche Untersuchungen zum Neuen Testament. Tübingen: Mohn Siebeck, 2013.

———. *Scripture Cannot Be Broken.* Leiden: E. J. Brill, 2003.

Coffin, William Sloane. *Credo.* Louisville, KY: Westminster John Knox Press, 2004. Kindle edition.

Coloe, Mary. *God Dwells with Us: Temple Imagery in the Gospel of John.* Wilmington, DE: Michael Glazier, 2001.

Daniel, John. *Of Earth: New and Selected Poems.* Sandpoint: ID: Lost Horse Press, 2012.

Garroway, Joshua D. "*Ioudaios.*" In *The Jewish Annotated New Testament,* edited by Amy-Jill Levine and Marc Z. Brettler. 524–26. New York: Oxford University Press, 2011.

Levine, Amy-Jill. *The Misunderstood Jew: The Church and the Scandal of the Jewish Jesus*. New York: HarperOne, 2007.
Martyn, J. Louis. *History and Theology in the Fourth Gospel*. Rev. and Exp. New Testament Library. Louisville, KY: Westminster John Knox Press, 2003.
Meeks, Wayne A. "The Image of the Androgyne." *History of Religions* 13 (1974): 165–208.
Melcher, Sarah J., Mikeal C. Parsons, and Amos Yong, eds. *Disability and the Bible: A Commentary*. Waco, TX: Baylor University Press, forthcoming.
Mitchell, David T. and Sharon L. Snyder. *Narrative Prosthesis: Disability and the Dependencies of Discourse*. Ann Arbor: University of Michigan Press, 2000.
Moloney, Francis J. *The Gospel of John*. Sacra Pagina, vol. 4. Collegeville, MN: Liturgical, 1998.
Moore, Stephen E. *Post-structuralism and the New Testament*. Minneapolis: Fortress, 1994.
Oliver, Mary. *House of Light*. Boston: Beacon Press, 1990.
Reinhartz, *Befriending the Beloved Disciple: A Jewish Reading of the Gospel of John*. New York: Bloomsbury Academic, 2002.
———. "John." In *The Jewish Annotated New Testament*, edited by Amy-Jill Levine and Marc Z. Brettler. 152–96. New York: Oxford University Press, 2011.
Salmon, Marilyn. *Preaching without Contempt: Overcoming Unintended Anti-Judaism*. Minneapolis: Fortress, 2006.
Schneiders, Sandra. *Written That You May Believe*. New York: Crossroad, 2003.
Silverstein, Shel. *Where the Sidewalk Ends*. New York: Harper and Row, 1974.
Taylor, Beth. "Movement toward the Light: Nicodemus and Becoming a Child of God." Unpublished paper, Perkins School of Theology, December 5, 2014.
Trible, Phyllis. *God and the Rhetoric of Sexuality*. Philadelphia: Fortress, 1978.
The Visual Bible: The Gospel of John. DVD. Directed by Philip Saville. Toronto: Think Film, 2003.
von Wahlde, Urban. *The Gospel and Letters of John*. 3 vols. Grand Rapids: Eerdmans, 2010.
———. "'The Jews' in the Gospel of John: Fifteen Years of Research (1983-1998)." *Ephemerides Theologicae Lovanienses* 76 (2000): 30–55.
———. "The Johannine 'Jews': A Critical Survey." *New Testament Studies* 28 (1982): 33–60.
Wolff, Tobias. *The Vintage Book of American Short Stories*. New York: Vintage Contemporaries, 1994.
Wynn, Kerry H. "Johannine Healings and the Otherness of Disability." *Perspectives in Religious Studies* 34 (2007): 61–75.

Index

CPSIA information can be obtained
at www.ICGtesting.com
Printed in the USA
LVHW020149130423
744267LV00014B/595